D1530907

Twayne's English Authors Series

Sylvia E. Bowman, *Editor*

INDIANA UNIVERSITY

Wyndham Lewis

(TEAS) 65

Wyndham Lewis

By WILLIAM H. PRITCHARD

Amherst College

Twayne Publishers, Inc. :: New York

And then one day Mr. Lewis who had penetrated into my drawing room office with all the aspects of a Russian conspirator-spy . . . Mr. Wyndham Lewis (Percy) caught me mysteriously by the elbow, willed me out into Holland Street and, in his almost inaudible voice . . . said it. . . .

"You and Mr. Conrad and Mr. James and all those old fellows are done. . . . Exploded! . . . *Fichus!* . . . *Vieux jeu!* . . . No good! . . . Finished! . . . Look here! . . . You old fellows are merely nonsensical. You go to infinite pains to get in your conventions. . . . *Progression d'effets.* . . . *Charpentes.* . . . Time-shift. . . . God knows what. . . . And what for? What in Heaven's name for? You want to kid people into believing that, when they read your ingenious projections they're actually going through the experiences of your characters. Verisimilitude—that's what you want to get with all your wheezy efforts. . . . But that isn't what people want. They don't want vicarious experience; they don't want to be educated. They want to be amused. . . . By brilliant fellows like me. Letting off brilliant fireworks. Performing like dogs on tight ropes. Something to give them the idea they're at a performance. You fellows try to efface yourselves; to make people think that there isn't any author and that they're living in the affairs you . . . adumbrate, isn't that your word? . . . What balls! What rot! . . . What's the good of being an author if you don't get any fun out of it? . . . Efface yourself! . . . Bilge!"

I often wonder what fun Mr. Lewis has got out of being an author since those old days.

FORD MADOX FORD in *Portraits From Life*

Preface

My aim in this study is to present Wyndham Lewis as a novelist and critic of modern culture; to demonstrate through quotation, comment, and analysis the significant life of his most interesting books; and to place those books within the temporal and imaginative sequence of a literary career extending from 1909 to 1956. It is hard to think of a comparable modern imagination that spans those fifty years; although Lewis published over forty books during the span (to say nothing of his graphic work), and although in retrospect he admitted that some of them were slight or haphazard or both, I am less interested in reproving him for writing too much too hastily than in making the necessary distinctions of importance and value among the books he wrote.

Although the reader is not expected to acquiesce in my claim for Lewis' greatness as a writer, it should be made clear just what that claim is. He wrote no single realized creative masterpiece of the stature of James Joyce's *Ulysses,* D. H. Lawrence's *Women in Love,* or T. S. Eliot's *Four Quartets;* and, invoking Eliot's remark about Shakespeare, it is only when we consider Lewis' works as forming a single work that his full imaginative value can be appreciated. The writer who never produced a masterpiece is nonetheless a writer of masterly significance. Rather than dealing with Lewis as D. H. Lawrence was dealt with for years—as a sick writer of "genius" whose genius was beyond analysis but whose sickness could be deplored at length—I propose to compare him with other modern British writers of the highest order: with Joyce or W. B. Yeats or Eliot or Lawrence, that is, rather than with E. M. Forster, Virginia Woolf, or Ford Madox Ford. I use the word "writer" rather than "novelist" because the novel is only one, though the most important one of Lewis' many performances as a man of words. And this already selective treatment offers only a cursory consideration of his impressive work as a painter and as a publicist for the Vorticist revolution in modern art.

The publication of Lewis' letters, imaginatively edited by W. K. Rose, enables us to supplement and correct what we already know about his life. Mr. Rose's editorial notes and interspersed commentary are of such high quality that the lack of any biography of Lewis matters less than it otherwise would. My debt to this edition of the letters is second only to that which I owe Hugh Kenner's *Wyndham Lewis* (1954) which first formulated a case for Lewis' importance that has never been challenged, though it has been sometimes overlooked. My disagreements with Mr. Kenner are trivial, compared to my sympathy with the large outlines of his argument and my admiration for the brilliance of his particular insights. But I think it is time for another attempt to see Lewis' career in its progression and its wholeness.

Page references to Lewis' work have been inserted directly into the text when it is clear what book is being referred to. When there is more than one edition of a particular work, the edition used is designated by an asterisk beside it in the bibliography. In certain places the abbreviations *L* and *RA* designate *The Letters of Wyndham Lewis*, and his retrospective memoir *Rude Assignment*. I am grateful to Mrs. Wyndham Lewis and to Mr. George Healey of the Cornell University Library for permission to quote from the Wyndham Lewis Archive at Cornell; also to Methuen and Co., Ltd., London, for permission to quote from the following books by Wyndham Lewis: *Tarr, Time and Western Man, The Wild Body, The Revenge for Love, The Human Age*, and *The Letters of Wyndham Lewis;* also to Henry Regnery Company for permission to quote from Lewis' *The Revenge for Love, Rotting Hill*, and *Self Condemned;* also to New Directions for permission to quote from *The Letters of Wyndham Lewis* and Hugh Kenner's *Wyndham Lewis*.

I wish to thank President Calvin H. Plimpton and the Trustees of Amherst College for granting me a fellowship which allowed me to write the major portion of this book. I also wish to thank the American Council of Learned Societies and The American Philosophical Association for their generous financial assistance.

Mrs. Muriel Crosson and Mrs. Jean Dunbar admirably typed various versions of this manuscript; my thanks to them, and to

Preface

William W. Heath and George Kateb who read and criticized an earlier version of the manuscript. To Benjamin DeMott, Robert Garis, Richard Poirier, and Roger Sale, none of them devoted readers of Wyndham Lewis, I am grateful for instructive argument about novels. And to Theodore Baird and G. Armour Craig I owe enough of my intellectual character to hold them responsible, however loosely, for my writing on Lewis at all.

Amherst College

WILLIAM H. PRITCHARD

Contents

Chronology

1882 Percy Wyndham Lewis born November 18 on his father's yacht moored near Amherst, Nova Scotia.

1893 Lewis' parents separate; he lives for some years with his mother in London suburbs.

1897– Lewis attends Rugby; ranks twenty-sixth in a class of
1898 twenty-six.

1898– Pupil at Slade School of Art. Writes poetry; meets Sturge
1901 Moore and Lawrence Binyon.

1902– Residing mainly in Paris. Visits Spain, Germany; spends
1908 summers in Brittany. Friendship with Augustus John.

1909 Return to England. First stories appear in *English Review*. Tries to publish potboiling novel.

1909– Associated with various art movements. Becomes closely
1913 involved with Ezra Pound as they publicize Vorticist revolution. Also meets Henri Gaudier-Breszka, Richard Aldington. Breaks with Roger Fry in 1913 and leads active opposition against him.

1914 *Blast*, "Review of the Great English Vortex," No. 1. Founded with Pound; edited and largely written by Lewis. Completes *Tarr*, a novel.

1915 *Blast*, No. 2. Contains Eliot's "Preludes" and "Rhapsody on a Windy Night."

1916 Enters military service in March, trained as gunner and bombardier. Receives commission and leaves for France in May of following year. *Tarr* begins serial publication in *The Egoist*.

1918 *Tarr* published.

1919 Returns to London; publishes *The Caliph's Design*, a plea for an ideal architecture.

1920– "Semi-retirement." Produces many drawings, edits art re-
1925 view *The Tyro*, Nos. 1, 2. Does much reading, works on

many books, contributes to Eliot's *Criterion* and to *The Calendar of Modern Letters.*

1926   *The Art of Being Ruled.* Beginning of great productive period of literature and criticism.

1927   *Time and Western Man: The Enemy,* Nos. 1 & 2, a literary-polemical review; *The Wild Body; The Lion and the Fox.* W. B. Yeats becomes an admirer.

1928   *The Childermass,* Part I; *Tarr,* thoroughly revised edition.

1929   *The Enemy,* No. 3; *Paleface.* Lewis, in private ceremony, marries Gladys Anne Hoskyns.

1930   *The Apes of God; Satire and Fiction.* Visits Germany.

1931   *The Diabolical Principle* and *The Dithyrambic Spectator; Hitler.* Travels in North Africa.

1932–   Period of frequent illness, many controversies. Three of
1936   Lewis' books withdrawn either before or after publication.

1932   *Snooty Baronet; The Doom of Youth.*

1934   *Men Without Art.*

1937   *The Revenge for Love; Blasting and Bombardiering;* Large exhibition of his paintings at the Leicester Galleries. "Wyndham Lewis Number" of *Twentieth Century Verse.*

1938   Lewis' portrait of T. S. Eliot refused by Royal Academy. Winston Churchill defends the Academy. Lewis writes of Churchill's "passionate advocacy of platitude."

1939–   In United States (Buffalo, New York, Long Island) until
1945   November 1940. In Canada (Toronto, Windsor) until August 1945. Lewis lectures for a year at Assumption College and spends part of 1944 in St. Louis.

1941   *The Vulgar Streak.*

1945   Returns to London to reside mainly at Notting Hill Gate.

1946–   Art critic for *The Listener* until failure of eyesight.
1951

1950   *Rude Assignment.*

1951   *Rotting Hill;* British Broadcasting Company radio version of *The Childermass.* Granted a small pension by government. Failure of sight; gives up art reviewing.

1952   *The Writer and the Absolute;* awarded D. Litt., University of Leeds.

1953   Lewis totally blind.

1954   *Self Condemned.*

Chronology

1955   *The Human Age.*
1956   Tate Gallery Retrospective Exhibition: "Wyndham Lewis and Vorticism."
1957   Died March 1.

CHAPTER 1

A Career of Performances

IN a dark moment in 1948 Wyndham Lewis predicted, with the accuracy of fantasy, how things would turn out after his demise: "My books afterwards would be shared out among various writers. D. B. W. L. would get two or three more, Day Lewis be given a couple probably and the *screw-tape* Lewis have attributed to him 'Time and Western Man.' Were I not to expire . . . and should I, the war over at last, return to London, I might be regarded as an embarrassing revenant." Lewis thought himself, rightly so, a master of the informal style; and this casual remark is as revealing of his character as we could possibly wish. A reader who has heard unpleasant tales of the self-righteous or vindictive streak in Lewis' nature might find confirmation in remarks such as this one; for, even if it is understood that D. B. W. L. (Dominick Bevan Wyndham Lewis) was a contemporary English writer whom Wyndham Lewis was anxious not to be confused with, there still remains a somewhat churlish self-regard that we may find difficult to associate with our image of the free-spirited writer who, of course, should rise above such things.

The thing to be said first is that in one sense Lewis never did rise above such things: his letters, his quarrels with all and sundry, his endless justification of self and recriminations toward others—these are a central aspect of his literary and personal career. It would be tempting, in the interests of pure literary criticism, to brush them aside and claim that only in his writings are such personal considerations transcended and the best self of Wyndham Lewis revealed. They are, and it is; yet it would be false to pretend that life and work can so neatly be separated in a man whose whole effort of mind is to insist on their relatedness, and whose motives, for all his defense of the absoluteness of Art, had little in common with purely esthetic ones. Lewis, that is, was a moralist—however much he detested the word—and the passage quoted above points a moral. As evident from the scrutiny of Lewis' books in print, it has turned out still to be more or less the case twenty years later.

To return to the remark quoted above: it can indeed be taken as another one of Lewis' complaints about being neglected; it can also be admitted as to some extent true. But it is finally the peculiar brand of sardonic humor that distinguishes and marks it as Wyndham Lewis' own. The annoyance about sharing his name with others is brought out nicely in the casual, unrespectful movement from "D. B. W. L." to "Day Lewis" to, as a climax, "the *screw-tape* Lewis," as if it were hard to remember C. S. Lewis' initials and as if "*screw-tape* Lewis"—the philosopher, Christian apologist, and general meditator on man's problems—would of course be assumed to have written a book titled *Time and Western Man.* The writer's problems and annoyances have been transformed into the energy of a successful literary performance, the net effect of which is exhilaration rather than depression. It is a fine comic perception of the maddening fitness of things.

Ford Madox Ford's sense of Lewis, as expressed in the words he claims or imagines Lewis uttered—"They want to be amused . . . by brilliant fellows like me. . . . Something to give them the idea they're at a performance. . . ."—introduces a metaphor of performance wholly appropriate both to the character of Lewis' fiction and criticism, and to his whole literary career when seen in its largest, most striking outlines. Like the great Victorian sages— Arnold, Carlyle, and Ruskin in particular—Lewis, from the beginning of his literary effort, was out to put things right, to see objects as in themselves they really were (adapting Arnold's phrase about criticism), and to overwhelm, with all the verbal brilliance he could command, those tendencies in society and in the arts which he held in contempt and fear. But he is very much a twentieth-century sage insofar as he typically—though not always— was aware that the grand style of English castigation had been exploited by earlier writers to the point where it might well fall on deaf ears unless made new and supple. Lewis made it new by imposing his own idiosyncratic and aggressive traits on the language and by becoming, in the words of one of his earliest stories, a soldier of humor. What he came to refer to, in an honorific way, as "coarseness," is a handy term for labeling the temperamental and stylistic quality that is ever apparent—for all the shades and discriminations that can be made—in his writing. Before making these discriminations, one should glance briefly at the sweep of Lewis' career. He was as a man and a writer very much of his time; and perhaps that is why he devoted so much energy to dispraising it.

I *Early Appearances, 1882–1909*

Mr. William Rose has uncovered the birth certificate establishing that Percy Wyndham Lewis was born on November 18, 1882 on his father's yacht, tied up near Amherst, Nova Scotia. In an unpublished memoir of his father titled *The Do-Nothing Mode,* Wyndham Lewis (he soon dropped the Percy) set out "to limn, as best I can, an American *eccentric:* for he was eccentric almost to the point of madness." [1] The evidence suggests that indeed Charles E. Lewis seems to have been an engaging and irresponsible character who spent a year at West Point, fought in the Civil War (about which he wrote a number of memoirs), and eventually married an English girl, Anne Stuart. When they separated in 1893, Mrs. Lewis settled in England with her son who then saw his father infrequently, although the latter did provide an uncertain amount of money for his son's education.

In terms of Lewis' own fiction, his father was a "wild body"; without intellectual direction, his career might be described as a comic venture from place to place. Yet this "American eccentric" had a way with language which, at least in the following remark from a letter to his brother, was unmistakably prophetic of a Wyndham Lewis performance: "I am bound to tell you that for many, many months past I have been engaged in a low kind of butcher business. Though the crime of which my conscience accuses me is not of an atrocious nature, nevertheless it is a case of killing. I have been killing TIME." [2] That the writer's son devoted so much of his career to killing Time in a rather different sense is no doubt coincidental; but the broad verbal delight with which Charles Lewis executed this confession is something Wyndham Lewis must have found very much to his taste.

Lewis attended Rugby, and studied at the Slade School of Art from 1898 to 1901. Aside from visits to Germany and Spain, he spent the years 1902–1909 being an artist in Paris and in Brittany. The Paris years and the Breton summers received their respective literary salutes in the two main books of Lewis' early career: *Tarr,* published in 1918 and revised in 1928, but actually written in 1914; and most of the stories in *The Wild Body* (1927), many of which appeared in different form as early as 1909 in Ford Madox Ford's *English Review*. Although the concerns of the young art student in Paris are clearly remote from the wordless heroes of his early stories, there exists an unmistakable continuity between Lewis in his letters and the colorful primitive—"The Pole"—of his first published story. For example, he writes to his mother asking advice on what to do with a packet of dirty clothes, requests that she send him slim volumes of poems by Lawrence Binyon and Sturge Moore, and then reveals that "I'm working hard and my bowels are open,—though I don't suggest any connection between two such independently amusing facts" (16–17). And while describing the character of a "Pole"—the outlandish hero of his early story—he is led to generalize, in the following description of a peculiar kind of humorist:

> The practical joker is a degenerate, who is exasperated by the uniformity of life. Or he is one who mystifies people, because only when suddenly perplexed or surprised do they become wildly and startlingly natural. He is a primitive soul, trying to get back to his element. Or it is the sign of a tremendous joy in people, and delight in seeing them put forth their vitality, and in practical joking of a physical nature a joy in the grotesqueness of the human form. Or it is the sadness of the outcast, the spirit outside of life because his nature is fit only for solitude, playing hobgoblin tricks with men that cannot sympathise with him. . . . The *farceur* has often many friends and admirers who brave the terrors of his friendship, but he remains peculiarly little understood. He is a lonely hero.[3]

The various possibilities—connected by the string of "or's"—do not exclude each other, and the whole passage is much more strongly imagined than the rather desultory tale in which it is placed. The passage reads like a prophetic foretelling of how Lewis' spirit was about to reveal itself in various guises over the next half-century. What the guises have in common is a self-dramatizing verve that is large enough to contain joy and sadness, society and solitude, by uniting them in the posture of the lonely hero.

II   *On Stage, 1909–1920*

Lewis returned to England in 1909, and in the following decade he emerged as a revolutionary artist, soldier, and novelist. In his letters of those years we can trace a history of affiliations and violent disjunctions; Lewis' most important friend and ally was, of course, Ezra Pound, with whom he collaborated in putting out two issues of the infamous *Blast*, the verbal and typographical fireworks of which announced the "Vorticist" revolution. Hugh Kenner has characterized Lewis' *Blast* style as the attempt "never again to write a phrase that will betray a hint of literary antecedents," and Kenner tells how this Vorticist prose set out to abolish time by violently conjoining words and phrases that had never been conjoined before; for example, the stars become "Throats iron eternities, drinking heavy radiance, limbs towers of blatant light, the stars poised, immensely distant, with their metal sides, pantheistic machines." [4] Kenner points out how this is a style "composed of phrases, not actions," and how it serves well only insofar as it doesn't try to express anything happening. Whether or not, as Kenner also argues, the Vorticist style should be emphasized as containing the germ of Lewis' future development as a novelist is debatable. My own instinct, with regard to Lewis' prose style, is to treat it as a voice rather than a machine, and to concentrate more on how we respond to it than on how it is put together.

At any rate, Lewis' literary beginnings in the period 1910–20 are conducted as a sideline, or even an afterthought, to more strenuous and engaging realities: his service in the war as an artillery man, his publicity campaigns for the avant-garde, his own graphic work. Even though he revised *Tarr* in 1928, it is still essentially a work of the previous decade. Appearing in *The Egoist* beginning in June 1916 and published in 1918, Lewis treats it in a letter to Augustus John (1914?) as an exercise in analytical psychology that makes no excessively literary claims: "The language is not travaillé: any beauty it may possess depending on the justness of the psychology,—as is the case in the Russian novels, I suppose. I think it is a great thing to have ready to one's hand a good many forms,—novel, jaunty or vernacular essay, story like Verlaine's. . . ." (65).

The young man's intention is to speak casually about his first

novel—especially since his audience is the free-swinging Augustus John—but Lewis' comment is accurate too. *Tarr* (in both versions) remains an attractively youthful and prewar book; like the
stories collected later in *The Wild Body*, it is high-spirited, sanguine about the possibilities for art, and breezily unpessimistic
about world conditions—cultural, artistic, or political. These characteristics never appeared together again in Lewis' work after
1920.

III *Playing All the Parts, 1920–1929*

From 1920 until the publication of *The Art of Being Ruled* in
1926, Lewis' career took place more or less underground. It is evident that he did an immense amount of reading, particularly of
those books that had shaped the contemporary mind of Europe, in
order to prepare himself for the task of explaining that contemporary mind to itself. His letters from the 1920's are almost exclusively concerned with work; from the correspondence with Eliot,
Robert McAlmon, and others, we learn that he was engaged in
writing a long book to be titled *The Man of the World*. Never
finished or published in this form, Lewis split it up into a number
of books; and it is therefore dangerous to distinguish the resultant
texts on the grounds of genre. If *The Childermass* and *The Apes
of God* are fiction, however uneasily we employ the term, what is
the right classification for *The Art of Being Ruled, Time and
Western Man,* or *The Lion and the Fox?* At any rate, the self that
produced these books is certainly most uncompromising and un-
appealing: incredibly suspicious, tight-lipped except when he is
tormenting an enemy, monumentally industrious. An economically hard-ridden survivor of World War I, Lewis surveyed modern ruins in his art, while in his criticism he tried to put a few of
them back together.

We see this suspiciousness quite frequently in those of his letters in which he tended to fall back on self-righteous superiority if
challenged about the lines his genius should follow. When the
solicitous Mr. Eliot, as editor of the *Criterion,* suggested with due
circumspection that Lewis should confine himself to one project at
a time, rather than taking on ten or eleven at once, his advice was
rejected without circumspection. The fact that Eliot had just referred to a section of what was to be *The Apes of God,* as a "mas-

terpiece" did not, in Lewis' hard head, allow him special privileges as a sage adviser. And Pound, who suggested that it might be time for a "Lewis number" of the *Little Review,* was told to mind his own business and not to presume that the atmosphere of the *Blast* days still existed. Only a true friend could have replied to Lewis' bullying the way Pound succeeded in doing as he wrote back that "There are some matters in which you really do behave like, and *some* (some not all) lines in this letter of yours in which you really do write like, a God damn fool."

With the advantage of hindsight we can see now that the "God damn fool" was about to publish *The Art of Being Ruled* and *Time and Western Man;* and Lewis made his own way toward the publication of these and other books of the late 1920's by using whatever strong personal means—aggressiveness, scorn, a high-spirited insistence on what his talents were worth—seemed appropriate for the occasion or for the specific person at hand. He worked his friends no harder than he worked himself, as a remark from a letter to Eliot implies: "I work incessantly at it. I am never in bed before 2, or often later; and for the present dine alone to get it done. This week I really think I shall be able to" (137).

The culminating event in this stage of Lewis' career was the publication in 1930 of *The Apes of God.* This immense satire had been in the making for six years, and was designed to overwhelm by sheer verbal power the shams of Bloomsbury-Bohemia. Lewis mounted a publicity campaign in regard to the book's publication and reception that put him in the center of things as he had not been since the days of *Blast.* But in an odd way this propaganda warfare succeeded too well for his own future as a literary figure. The relative neglect into which his work fell in the next decade can be accounted for not only simply because of the ill-advised *Hitler,* but because he was now typed as a bothersome and unpleasant satirist who could be most effectively reduced in influence by being ignored. And a number of sufficiently prominent literary people were eager to do just that. The result was, in part, that Lewis' writings during the 1930's show a somewhat frantic dispersion of energies. A continuing illness and its attendant financial strain contributed their bit to the frustration and harassment testified to by the letters of this period; also, in response to the leftward movement of many British writers, Lewis perversely

simplified his own politics and became more shrilly rightist in his
role as the man of peace who condoned or ignored some very
warlike manifestations in Germany.

The best evidence that all was not well within the writer can be
found in the often strident uncertainty of the books themselves
about what kind of audience they aspire to, or even about who,
possibly, in the world, they might reach. The arrogantly highbrow
artist of *The Childermass* or of *The Apes of God;* the forceful
intellectual of *Time and Western Man;* and the disengaged creator of *Tarr* and *The Wild Body*—all largely disappear. In their
place we hear a voice that often sounds like that of a genial American gangster: "You may have heard of the Jesuits. They were a
lot of priests (there are still a lot of them), they belonged to the
Roman communion and wished the Pope to be very powerful. . . . They were awfully clever guys and a bit sly. . . .
And they saw to it that they were given all the babies piping-hot
out of the cradles (for the Pope was very strong still in those
days. . . .)" [5] Such talk has little usefulness for the reader who
doesn't need to be reminded how strong the Pope was in those
days; and the wit is not of matchless quality. Of course, this
particular passage represents Lewis at his worst, and the decade
includes the virtually unnoticed publication of his best novel, *The
Revenge for Love.*

Nor is it true that his reputation went into utter eclipse. In 1937
he was paid intelligent tribute by a number of writers, most of
them younger ones, in Julian Symons' magazine *Twentieth Century Verse.* Among the contributors of mainly laudatory pieces
were Julian and his brother A. J. A. Symons, Hugh Gordon Porteus, Ruthven Todd, the music critic Constant Lambert, G. W.
Stonier, D. S. Savage, and Rex Warner. Neither a Bloomsbury nor
an academic group, it seemed to have no demonstrable political
line (an achievement in itself in 1937), nor any interest in praising or dispraising Lewis' rightist allegiances. In some ways the
group resembles the highly publicized if vaguely defined "movement" writers of the England of the 1950's: strongly journalistic in
flavor, and ready to talk on all subjects in the same no-nonsense
colloquial tone. If Kingsley Amis or John Wain were transposed
back to 1937, they might perhaps have contributed to the issue.
The interesting thing is that Lewis, then fifty-five years old,

figured momentarily as the respectable elder statesman of a "movement" that never realized itself.

IV *Some Final Roles, 1940–1957*

By 1939, oppressed with debts incurred during his illness, and despairing over the life of an artist in England during the coming war, Lewis sailed for Canada with his wife, hoping to support himself there and in the United States by painting portraits. What happened in fact can be seen from the long and exceptionally fascinating group of letters from these years, as well as in the monument Lewis gave this period of his life in his late novel *Self Condemned.* He painted, lectured, and taught, but did almost no formal literary work during the exile; it is not surprising then that the letters take on self-revelatory aspects largely absent from those which precede them.

Reading through these letters is a painful and unforgettable experience, partly because their tone so largely contradicts the alternately jocular or icy one of the aggressive Enemy met with earlier. A letter to James Johnson Sweeney written in 1940 sets the note of many to follow, as Lewis speaks of his inability to find a New York publisher for his novel *The Vulgar Streak,* then mentions his lack of success in arranging lecture dates or journalistic work or a gallery show, and finally concludes: "—When you read me that letter the other night I found myself envying James Joyce at Vichy—so much nearer the centre of his world and of mine: with so many more friends than I have too, within some sort of reach. I feel as if I were in a stony desert, full of shadows, in human form. I have never imagined the likes of it, in my worst nightmares" (277). The months spent in what Lewis referred to as the "sanctimonious icebox" of Toronto were a time of boredom and frustration almost beyond the reach of his own irony.

Perhaps the sharpest adjustment Lewis made was a political one. He concerned himself with justifying his political position during the last ten years, but also repudiated that position in the light of what he now believed would emerge from the war. Some sentences from a letter to Naomi Mitchison put this belief succinctly: "Our tribe [England] had suffered terribly the last time it went to war: when I heard the war-drums rolling again I was almost madly concerned. I turned upon the leftwing you remember, because it seemed to be from that quarter that the war-psychosis came.—It is now apparent to me that I thought too much of our tribe: too little of the 'genre humain.' . . . The benefits that may—or we must say *shall*—ensue for the genre humain as a result of this war are incalculable" (328). He then praises Roosevelt, global centralization, and the idea of one world.

Although the sentiments are admirable enough, Lewis the novelist had difficulty making immediate use of them; for, by becoming a universalist, a supporter of the "genre humain," he was inevitably to face the problem of just what kind of fiction was worth writing in the new age to come. Not until a decade or so later, with the publication of *Self Condemned* and *The Human Age*, did he manage to find a compelling literary way of expressing his concern for Man, as well as his exasperations toward men.

Unlike the hero of *Self Condemned* who accepts a meaningless job in an American university after his wife commits suicide in Canada, Lewis returned to England with his wife, reestablished himself in Notting Hill, and lived there to face his gradual loss of sight along with, more cheerfully, a certain amount of artistic and literary recognition. The controversialist lashed out at his enemies as if he had never left home, but the naturally retrospective tenor of his letters and of the autobiographical *Rude Assignment* impresses the reader with its candor and speculativeness. Correspondence with Eliot and Pound picked up again; and, in general, his range of subjects and of friends was gratifyingly wide. For the first time in his career we have the sense that Lewis is writing only what he most deeply wants to, out of the center of himself.

There is much that is attractive about completing our discussion of Lewis' life and character with another reference to the description of the "Pole" he had written fifty years earlier: "The *farceur* has often many friends and admirers who brave the terrors of his friendship, but he remains peculiarly little understood. He is a lonely hero." The fact that this lonely hero was now blind makes the dramatic situation undeniably affecting. When Lewis was forced to cease reviewing art exhibitions for *The Listener* in 1951, he took leave of his audience with a sentence that has been often quoted: "Pushed into an unlighted room, the door banged and locked forever, I shall then have to light a new lamp in my mind to keep at bay the night." But, as no one knew better than he, Lewis was not John Milton nor was meant to be; we need to complement the heroic image of keeping "at bay the night" with an equally vital one which appears earlier in that same valedictory, and which describes what a nearly blind man does by day:

Sometimes I am still at large solo, though increasingly rarely. I may go out, for instance, and some twenty yards away look for a taxicab. In these cases I will stand upon the edge of the pavement, calling imperiously to owner-drivers "Are you *free?*" who observe me coldly from behind their steering-wheels as if I were the Yonghi-Bonghi Bo. I signal small vans, I peer hopefully at baby trucks. . . . At length I get a response. It *is* a taxi. But I assure you that it is one thing to hail a taxi-cab, another to get into it. This is quite extraordinarily difficult. I try to force my way in beside the indignant driver. He or I will open the door. But as I see everything so indistinctly I attempt to effect a passage through the wood of the door itself, in Alice Through the Looking Glass fashion, rather than take advantage of the gaping hole in the side of the taxi produced by the opening of the door.[6]

If he is keeping "at bay the night," he is also, by day, the Yonghi-Bonghi-Bo, peering incompetently at small vans and calling out, as he has been calling out all his life, "Are you *free?*" It is fitting and appropriate that his audience take no more notice of him than they ever did. But the reader can listen and can feel particularly full satisfaction in the scene's final touch, where Lewis fails to enter a taxi by taking advantage of "the gaping hole in the side of the taxi." It is a representative and exemplary moment in Lewis' writings for the way it enables us, as any good writing does, to extend ourselves in ways previously unimagined and to take in an experience for which we had only the most settled and embarrassed names.

CHAPTER 2

The Satirist's Curse of Humor

I Principles and Techniques of Satire

> In *Tarr* I had in view a publique d'élite who
> could be addressed in blank verse, and the
> style of the poème en prose might suddenly be
> used, or be employed for half a page.
> . . . In writing *Tarr* I wanted at the same
> time for it to be a novel, and to do a piece
> of writing worthy of the hand of the abstractist
> innovator (which was an impossible combina-
> tion). Anyhow it was my object to eliminate
> anything less essential than a noun or a verb.
> Prepositions, pronouns, articles—the small fry
> —as far as might be, I would abolish. Of course
> I was unable to do this, but for the purposes
> of the *novel*, I produced a somewhat jagged
> prose.
>
> Wyndham Lewis, in a letter to
> Hugh Kenner, 1953

MOST readers who decide to approach Wyndham Lewis' novels usually begin with *Tarr*, and the first page of the original version published in 1918 provides immediate confirmation of
what they have probably heard—*Tarr* is avant-garde literature
that now seems decidedly like a period piece. The opening paragraph of the novel does not exactly hold the promise of an excit-
ing tale to follow: "Paris hints of sacrifice. = But here we deal
with that large dusty facet known to indulgent and congruous
kind. It is in its capacity of delicious inn and majestic Baedeker,
where western Venuses twang its responsive streets, and hush to
soft growl before its statues, that it is seen. It is not across its
Thébaïde that the unscrupulous heroes chase each other's shadows. They are largely ignorant of all but their restless personal
lives."

The single typographical innovation (=) recurs with varying degrees of frequency throughout the book. Its purpose may well have been, as Hugh Kenner suggests, to break up the flow of the prose; but the reader, unlikely to grasp that purpose, may well wonder why the device should follow or precede one sentence rather than another. At any rate, Lewis eliminated it in the revised (1928) version of the novel and smoothed out the "somewhat jagged prose" by the addition of a more conventional novelistic syntax that works through grammatical connectives and continuous paragraphing. At the same time the style is thickened and enriched by drawing out the implications of metaphors and by the writer's increased willingness to tell us about his characters: what they look like, what they are comparable with.

One representative passage suffices to establish the difference between the two versions and to make the case for treating the revised text as superior. In the earliest pages of the book, Tarr confronts a fellow "artist," Mr. Alan Hobson, who is first presented through his contemptible sartorial habit:

This was Alan Hobson's outfit. = A Cambridge cut disfigured his originally manly and melodramatic form. His father was a wealthy merchant at the Cape. He was very athletic, and his dark and cavernous features had been constructed by Nature as a lurking place for villainies and passions. But he slouched and ambled along, neglecting his muscles: and his dastardly face attempted to portray delicacies of commonsense, and gossamer-like backslidings into the Inane, that would have puzzled a bile-specialist. He would occasionally exploit his blackguardly appearance and blacksmith's muscles for a short time, however. And his strong, piercing laugh threw A.B.C. waitresses into confusion.

The Art-touch was very observable. Hobson's Harris tweeds were shabby. A hat suggesting that his ancestors had been Plainsmen or some rough sunny folk, shaded unnecessarily his countenance, already far from open.

([1918] 16–17)

But for Hobson's outfit Tarr had the most elaborate contempt. This was Alan Hobson's outfit: a Cambridge cut disfigured his originally manly and melodramatic form. His father was said to be a wealthy merchant somewhere in Egypt. Very athletic, his dark and cavernous features had been constructed by nature as a lurking-place for villainies and passions: but Hobson had double-crossed his rascally sinuous body. He slouched and ambled along, neglecting his muscles: and his full-blooded blackguard's countenance attempted to portray delicacies of common sense and gossamer-like backslidings into the inane that would have puzzled any analyst unacquainted with his peculiar training. Occasionally he would exploit his criminal appearance and blacksmith's muscles for a short time, however: and his strong piercing laugh threw A B C waitresses into confusion. The art-touch, the Bloomsbury technique, was very noticeable. Hobson's Harris tweeds were shabby, from beneath his dejected jacket emerged a pendant seat, his massive shoes were hooded by the superfluous inches of his trousers: a hat suggesting that his ancestors had been Plainsmen or some rough sunny folk shaded unnecessarily his countenance, already far from open.

([1928] 3–4)

Although both passages share a similarly detached air, the revised version is less abrupt and its rhythm more satisfying. No longer is the narrator simply concerned with laying down the strokes that create Hobson; he now combines them into a connected, reasonably syntactical paragraph that has beginning and end, and that brings a rhythm to completion. In the 1928 version Lewis is both confident about what his prose is doing and at ease in his relations with the reader; he has become the novelist rather than the abstractist innovator in prose.

There is no reason to dispute his own account of this change, recorded many years later in *Rude Assignment*. Speaking of the composition of *Tarr*, Lewis tells us that, in the days of *Blast* and the Vorticist revolution, he found most of his literary companions too bookish and that *Tarr* and his play *The Enemy of the Stars* were attempts to command a prose that would keep step with the revolutionary visual art he was producing. But he continues: "It became evident to me at once, however, when I started to write a novel, that words and syntax were not susceptible of transformation into abstract terms, to which process the visual arts lent themselves quite readily. The coming of war and the writing—at top-speed—of a full-length novel ('Tarr') was the turning-point. Writing—literature—dragged me out of the abstractist cul-de-sac" (129).

Lewis' style in the passage quoted above may be distinguished in one particular respect from the styles of some earlier English novelists with whom he has evident affinities. The "elaborate con-

tempt" Tarr displays toward Hobson is a characteristic shared
with his creator and one which can be found amply in the pages
of Dickens, Smollett, or Fielding. Lewis' originality in wielding
this contempt consists in making it as casual, off-hand, and deadpan as possible. The detached artist never stoops to crude insult or
to moralistic name-calling but makes it appear that his description of Hobson is simply the way Hobson *is*. Hobson's "double-
cross" of his own body is not a matter for approval or disapproval
by the narrator—he only observes what anyone can see merely by
looking. Of course, this observation is a trick; for none of us
but the artist sees not just long trousers and shoes, but "superfluous inches" of trousers that "hooded" the massive shoes.

When Ezra Pound in his review of *Tarr* praised Lewis' "highly
energized mind," [1] he probably had in mind the verbal energy
typified, in the passage about Hobson, by adjectives as strong as
"massive" or "superfluous" or "dejected" (for a jacket!). Lewis
himself, in his essay "Inferior Religions," published as a kind of
gloss to the stories in *The Wild Body*, says about the principles of
his own satire:

> I would present these puppets, then, as carefully selected specimens
> of religious fanaticism. With their attendant objects or fetishes they
> live and have a regular food and vitality. They are not creations, but
> puppets. You can be as exterior to them, and live their life as little,
> as the showman grasping from beneath and working about a Polichi-
> nelle. They are only shadows of energy, not living beings. Their mech-
> anism is a logical structure and they are nothing but that.
>
> Boswell's Johnson, Mr. Veneering, Malvolio, Bouvard and Pécuchet,
> the "commissaire" in *Crime and Punishment* do not live; they are con-
> gealed and frozen into logic, and an exuberant hysterical truth. They
> transcend life and are complete cyphers, but they are monuments of
> dead imperfection. Their only significance is their egoism. So the great
> intuitive figures of creation live with the universal egoism of the poet.
> This "Realism" is satire.
>
> (234–35)

Although it is a long way from Alan Hobson to any of these literary monuments mentioned by Lewis, it is as an exuberant, hysterical truth—a puppet—that Hobson is presented to us. Lewis the
showman, aided and abetted by Frederick Tarr—a showman in
his own right—puts Hobson through his paces; and, when this dis-

play of energy is finished, Tarr knocks his hat off, gives it a kick, and hurries away. The universal egoism of the poet has been satisfied momentarily.

In the above quotation from "Inferior Religions" Lewis insists at one moment that his "specimens of religious fanaticism" are puppets rather than creations, but he then claims Mr. Veneering, Malvolio, and the rest as "great intuitive figures of creation" who are archetypes of his own figures. There is no inconsistency if we realize that the showman is a creative artist who constructs puppets; shows the audience exactly what he wants them to see; and, in so doing, claims to be both realist and satirist. In discussing three distinguishing characteristics of pure Lewis satire as it is supposedly practiced in *Tarr* and in *The Wild Body*, we can suggest the superiority of the novel; for it is precisely because *Tarr* does not live up to the standards of pure satire as they are defined in *The Wild Body* that, as V. S. Pritchett suggested, it stands as a "considerable comic novel" [2] rather than as merely a period curiosity.

First, Lewis insists that the great "intuitive figures of creation" he has mentioned above transcend life, and are therefore beyond moral or social categories of judgment. This kind of satiric creation is akin to what T. S. Eliot admired in Dryden's poetry: its ability to "transform the object into something greater," and to "create the object" which it contemplates.[3] Indeed, MacFlecknoe and the famous plotters from *Absalom and Achitophel* could join Mr. Veneering and Malvolio as exuberant hysterical truths so thoroughly and overwhelmingly created through words that the reader is busy apprehending how the mechanism is put together rather than what vice or flaw he should laugh at.

In the stories of *The Wild Body* Lewis is the pure satirist, concerned only with putting together a mechanism—an exuberant, hysterical truth—and with presenting it for disinterested inspection. From the beginning of "Bestre" we have an athletic Frenchwoman on a cold day: "The crocket-like floral postiches on the ridges of her head-gear looked crisped down in a threatening way: her nodular pink veil was an apoplectic gristle round her stormy brow; steam came out of her lips upon the harsh white atmosphere. Her eyes were dark, and the contiguous colour of her cheeks of a redness quasi-venetian, with something like the feminine colouring of battle" (113). It is not surprising that the best

moments in these stories are crucial ones in which one or more
wild bodies like the Frenchwoman are caught up in the rhythm of
a dance and thereby fulfilled. At such a point the "story" can end
—narrative being but a means to push the bodies into contiguity,
then trigger the mechanism that sets them off. It is perhaps needless to say that a verbal art, operating on such principles and
standing at such distance from what we confidently call Life or
Reality, can have but a very special and limited appeal. The mar-
vel is not that the trick is done well but that it has been done at
all.

Second, Lewis makes it clear in "Inferior Religions" that he
looks upon these types of humanity as in fact violent individualities; therefore, Mr. Veneering belongs in the list not so much
as an "example" of the newly moneyed man moving up the social ladder, but, more primitively, as the intransigent possessor of
a set of "bran-new" furnishings, gestures, and language provided him by Dickens. In Lewis' case both the athletic Frenchwoman and Alan Hobson are violently individual; it would not
be satisfactory to say that the Hobson presented for our inspection "represents" or "is meant to satirize" Bloomsbury, or the
art touch, or even Cambridge sartorial habits; for the mechanism, the "individuality," is self-sufficient. There are many
other absurd individualities in the novel, but no one else's massive shoes are hooded by superfluous inches of trousers.

Finally, and closely allied to what has just been said, Lewis'
satire in its pure form is non-moral; or, stated in the most extreme terms employed by Lewis himself in *Men Without Art*,
"The Greatest Satire is Non-Moral." There is no essential contradiction between the argument of that later book and the one
found in *The Wild Body;* in each case, satire is "non-moral" in
that it works as a universal letdown for the species. In response
to the moralist defense that one only writes satire if the neglect
and abuse of virtue and truth compels one to do so, Lewis has
this to say: ". . . it is my belief that 'satire' *for its own sake*—
as much as anything else for its own sake—is possible; and that
even the most virtuous and well-proportioned of men is only a
shadow, after all, of some perfection; a shadow of an imperfect, and hence an 'ugly,' sort" (109). In this sense, he continues, either everybody or nobody should be laughed at. Non-
moral or "metaphysical" satire, Lewis argues, is both more

primitive and less crude than ethical satire: less crude in that there is no single moral code against which bad behavior is condemned; more primitive in that what he rather exclusively calls the "artistic" impulse is wayward, chancy, and various compared to the narrowly ethical bias of moral satire.

If we feel the presence of a straw man here, a definition of moral satire that unjustly reduces the artistic vigor of, say, Pope's *Moral Essays* to the simple promulgation of a code, the strongly drawn distinction still has value as an indication of what is to be met with in *Tarr* and the early stories. But, even at this stage in his career, Lewis found it much easier to keep his satire "pure" within the limits of a short story that turned on a single action or point than in that most impure of all forms, the novel. The writing of *Tarr* not only dragged Lewis out of the abstractist cul-de-sac, but showed that a writer who in his criticism was a strenuous moralist could not create a purely non-moral satire.

II   Tarr

Tarr has two heroes; and, since Ezra Pound's review, it has been customary to emphasize the second hero, the German Otto Kreisler, as the book's real achievement both in the independent solidity of his presence and in the vigorous rendering of his suicidal career. When Pound found Tarr rather too patently a mouthpiece for the author's opinions on art and life, Lewis took the criticism to heart, later called Tarr a "secondary figure," and said in *Rude Assignment* that the title should have born Kreisler's name instead. It is true that, quantitatively, the doings of Kreisler occupy the major part of the novel, also that there is a heavy intensity of presentation which contrasts with the more volatile and discontinuous portrayal of Tarr. But, without the presence of Tarr and the sections devoted to his sex troubles and his wit combats, the book would be intolerably heavy.

There is some danger as well that in admiring the novel which has gotten free of its creator—in the sense that no single character is the author's spokesman and therefore comparatively invulnerable to assault—we may condemn any such spokesman in any novel as a "failure," whether or not his opinions and statements contribute to the meaning of the book.

When Father Rothschild, the sage priest in Evelyn Waugh's *Vile Bodies,* indulges in sober lamentation on the rootless younger generation, it is both unnecessary and annoying, since the novel has shown this youth to us in a much more interesting way, and since Rothschild has largely been given immunity from Waugh's satirical thrusts. But that Rupert Birkin sounds like D. H. Lawrence is hardly a flaw in *Women in Love* since those beliefs and accents are a significant part of the novel's material for exploration and since they are far from immune to the sensible onslaughts of other characters in the book. Although Tarr shares little enough with Rupert Birkin, he too, in a much broader, more Shavian way, is finally taken to task by his author in the theatrical farce which ends the novel.

The events of *Tarr* are roughly as follows: after an evocation of the Parisian art quarter we meet Tarr, an Englishman and artist, engaged at present in straightening out his life—a messier problem than is art. Tarr solicits advice from and abuses three fellow artists—Hobson, Butcher, and Lowndes—then proceeds to Bertha Lunken, his German mistress. After a difficult and somewhat unsuccessful attempt to exorcise Bertha, Tarr leaves, supposedly bound for England. The next three sections of the novel deal almost wholly with Kreisler: his financial and sartorial embarrassments (he needs money from his father and a 'frac' for the evening's dance), his fascination with the newly met Anastasya Vasek, his debacle at the dance and attendant befriending by Bertha that culminates in a seduction-rape (with Kreisler we gather the distinctions are not drawn too nicely).

Soon Tarr reappears—not having gone to England after all —and, for no apparent reason, attaches himself to Kreisler. At the very point when it seems Kreisler must make some violent retaliation to this mysterious harassment, a fitter candidate for violence presents himself: the Pole, Soltyk, whom Kreisler has encountered with Anastasya and by whom he professes to have been insulted. While Tarr is forgotten, an elaborate and silly duel is arranged; Kreisler eventually shoots Soltyk, runs away, and finally gives himself up to the police at a town near the French-German border. He hangs himself in his cell; and his father, when notified, pays for the disposal of the body without comment. In the final section of the novel Tarr and Anastasya

work out, in the comic mode, their adjustment to each other.
But Bertha is pregnant by Kreisler, so Tarr gallantly splits his
personality, marries Bertha, and spends most of his time with
Anastasya. A coda to the novel reveals some future figures in
Tarr's marital and sexual career.

Pasting together the "plot" in this way shows how little the
interest of *Tarr* lies in a contrived sequence of events—in a
story; rather, the interest is indicated in a closing sentence from
the book's prefatory opening which refers to "unscrupulous
heroes" who are "largely ignorant of all but their restless personal lives." Restlessness and self-involvement characterize the
two heroes of the book, Tarr and Kreisler; the difference between them lies in the style with which each is presented. Tarr
is not only an artist but a self-styled philosopher-critic of manners, sex, laughter, work, and the English. As a showman, he
shares with his creator the gift of articulate speech; he is as ir-
repressibly talkative as one of Shaw's heroes; and, indeed, Tarr
bears a certain resemblance to Jack Tanner.

Both Tarr and Tanner spend much time and energy in hold-
ing life at bay, and they do so mainly through talk. Lewis says
of Tarr's conversation, abundantly featured in the opening sections of the book, that "It was a tribunal to which he brought
his hesitations" (20). On the way to Bertha's flat for a crucial
interview, Tarr expounds to Hobson the creative artist's sepa-
ration from life and sex: ". . . one by one his powers are
turned away from the usual object of a man's personal poetry
or passion and so removed from the immediate world. One soli-
tary thing is left facing any woman with whom he has com-
merce, that is his sex, a lonely phallus" (12). Or Tarr preaches
to the more sympathetic Guy Butcher a sermon on English humor and how it paralyzes the sense of reality. These outpourings
are attractive and amusing, sharply formulated and winningly
expressed. They are also exceedingly vulnerable in the rigidity
with which they draw hard lines between Art over here and
Life over there. Both Tarr and Lewis are conscious that the
large pronouncements are experimental, that hesitancies and
uncertainties underlie them.

But the comparison with Shaw breaks down when it is realized how much of the character, Tarr, is unexpressed in his
conversation and exists only through the medium of Lewis' ex-

traordinary prose, the effect of which is to render kinds of psychological combinations and balances of impressions that make up the book's strangeness and individuality. At the same time, these renderings stubbornly defeat a reader impatient for the novelist to get on with his story; for there is very little story apart from shifting prose constellations of gesture and attitude. Our sense of a "character" is inseparable from apprehending the medium.

This formal characteristic can be seen more clearly by looking at the writing about Tarr at two points in the book, the first of which describes his leaving Bertha. He has proceeded to her flat determined to test the staying power of his recently proclaimed indifference to life, putting at stake his integrity as an artist. The test fails by the end of the scene as Tarr realizes he is not immune to life's vulgar claims. Although Bertha's salon is the perfect bourgeois-bohemian interior and as such to be despised—"Green silk cloth and cushions of various vegetable and mineral shades covered everything in mildewy blight. The cold repulsive shades of Islands of the Dead, gigantic cypresses, grottoes of teutonic nymphs, had installed themselves massively in this french flat" (41)—Tarr's detachment is not sufficient to save him from being swayed by it: "She had loved him with all this: he had been loved with the plaster cast of Beethoven, this gentle girl had attacked him with the Klingers, had ambushed him from the Breton jars, in a funny superficial absorbing way" (67).

The concluding adjectives set the appropriate tone of regard for this event because we know, as does Tarr, that to put bad art and life together in this fashion is indeed funny, superficial, and absorbing; this is what it means to be loved with the plaster cast of Beethoven that was previously regarded with a colder eye, or to be ambushed from the Breton jars by a gentle girl. Momentarily, Lewis, Tarr, and the reader merge in a complicated state of balanced acceptance; attitudes are not to be taken toward an event that asks only to be contemplated through verbal possession. Nothing much happens between Tarr and Bertha; the interest of the scene lies wholly in the expressive use made of Tarr's consciousness. As a preparation for the anticlimactic "I am going now," signaling his departure, we find the following paragraph:

He had stirred up and brought out into the light during the last hour every imaginable difficulty, and created a number of new ones. They were there in a confused mass before him. The thought of "settling everything before he went" now appeared fantastic. He had at all events started these local monsters and demons, fishing them out stark where they could be seen. Each had a different vocal explosiveness or murmur, inveighing unintelligibly against the other. The only thing to be done was to herd them all together and march them away for inspection at leisure. Sudden herdsman, with the care of a delicate and antediluvian flock; well!—but what was Bertha to be told? Nothing. He would file out silently with his flock, without any horn-blasts or windings such as he customarily affected.

(68)

Yet the "horn-blasts and windings" are there in the prose and give it a peculiar mass and elaboration seen earlier in the Hobson passage. We are not challenged by an assertion or by a proposition but are invited to apprehend the thing—the state of things—for what it is. Lewis' task, while cooperating with his hero, is to present the showman disowning his own tricks while making use of them for our benefit.

The second passage has an autobiographical resonance and indicates the special sense in which Tarr is a "self-portrait" of Lewis. There are moments in the book when such resonance is felt, but the movement is outward, toward the encompassing of a general point or truth, rather than inward to psychological revelation. The narrative is not "external"—Lewis' word for describing his favorite approach to material—since it has a unity of effect that resists classification as either external or internal. Tarr and Anastasya promenade in the Luxembourg Gardens; and, after some strokes which render the look of the park to an objective observer, Lewis focuses on its significance for our hero:

This place represented the richness of three wasted years, three incredibly gushing, thick years—what had happened to this delightful muck? He had just turned seventeen when he had arrived there, and had wandered in this children's outdoor nursery almost a child himself. All this profusion had accomplished for him was to dye the avenues of a Park with personal colour for the rest of his existence. No one, he was quite convinced, had squandered so much of the imaginative stuff of life in the neighborhood of these terraces, ponds, and lawns.

So this was more nearly *his Park* than it was anybody else's: he should
never walk through it without bitter and soothing recognition from it.
Well, that was what the "man of action" accomplished. In four idle
years he had been, when most inactive, experimenting with the man
of action's job. He had captured a Park!—well! he had spent himself
into the earth, the trees had his sap in them.

He remembered a day when he had brought a newly purchased
book to the bench there, his mind tearing at it in advance, almost
writing it in its energy. He had been full of such unusual abounding
faith: the streets around these gardens, in which he had lodged alternately, were so many confluents and tributaries of memory, charging
in upon it on all sides with defunct puissant tides. The places, he then
reflected, where childhood has been spent, or where, later, dreams of
energy have been flung away, year after year, are obviously the health-
iest spots for a person where such places exist: but perhaps, although
he possessed the Luxembourg Gardens so completely, they were completely possessed by thousands of other people! So many men had
begun their childhood of ambition in this neighborhood. His hopes,
too, no doubt, had grown there more softly because of the depth and
richness of the bed. A sentimental miasma made artificially in Paris
a similar good atmosphere where the mind could healthily exist as was
found by artists in brilliant, complete and solid times. Paris was the
most human city we had.

(245–46)

The benign irony of this passage, proceeding from the impul-
sive "his park" to the reflection that the place is wonderful for
the way it allows one to claim possession of it, can only be accomplished through a character who is held in affection by his
creator. But, alongside this affection, certain words and phrases
harshen the sympathetic atmosphere and forestall any possibilities of dreamy identification with Tarr, either on Lewis' part
or on that of a reader anxious for such security. Three rich
wasted years are also "delightful muck"; the attractiveness of
Paris is also "sentimental miasma." To invest imaginatively in a
place is also to squander the stuff of life.

In general, the exclamatory air of these realizations, the obvious pleasure taken in turning on one's own monomania, and
the memorable sharpness of a mind "tearing" at a book in advance—all combine to make up what, perhaps as a sop to the
hesitant reader, Pound referred to in his review as "something
active and disagreeable" in Lewis' style. In fact, the writing

represents a particularly successful balance of rival claims: private experience and public reality, nature and human nature.

No such balance of impressions can occur, however, in the presentation of Otto Kreisler. Lewis tells us in *Rude Assignment* that this condemned hero "is expected to awaken neither sympathy nor repulsion in the reader—for it is not a moral tale: he is a *machine* (a 'puppet,' not a 'nature'), aloof and violent. His death is a tragic game" (151). This statement does not mean, contrary to a common assumption about Lewis' art, that Kreisler is set forth in purely visual or external images. We are told what goes on "inside" the character; but, since the character is a puppet, he is predictably inflexible and monolithic in his responses. If Hobson is all conventionally English humor, Kreisler just as conventionally lacks any humor. His mode of self-contemplation is that of angry bitterness; he operates by pushing himself and others around until some sort of collision, more or less violent, occurs.

V. S. Pritchett says flatly that, in creating Kreisler, Lewis had in fact created Hitler;[4] Lewis in retrospect compares him to Goebbels. What these analogies leave out is the fine comic possibilities open to the novelist in manipulating a puppet whose reality cannot be evident to himself. The *tour de force* of the novel and the apotheosis of Kreisler occur at the Bonnington Club dance when Anastasya laughs at him. He reacts typically by moving his body in the direction of a third party, in this case the widow Mrs. Bevelage and to the strains of the "Merry Widow"(!) the dance begins. As they approach the hostess Fraulein Liepmann, leader of the whole bourgeois-bohemian circle, Kreisler winks at her, then

Dancing very slowly, mournfully even, he and his partner bumped into her each time as they passed: each time it was a deliberate collision. Thud went the massive buffers of the two ladies. The widow felt the impact, but it was only at the third round that she perceived the method presiding at these bumps. She then realized that they were without fail about to collide with the other lady once more: the collision could not be avoided, but she shrank away, made herself as small as possible, bumped gently and apologized over her shoulder, with a smile and screwing up of her eyes, full of dumb worldly significance.
(163)

The motion has its expected outcome as the merry widow is eventually bumped down, her dress ripped in the process; Kreisler is accused of drunkenness, trades insults with Fraulein Liepmann, is overwhelmed by Anastasya's laughter, and leaves. There is little in the physical happening—the repeated collisions leading to a grand bump—that is particularly new to the English novel; but the scene ranks with the meeting of Bertie Stanhope, Mrs. Proudie, and the sofa in Trollope's *Barchester Towers*, as one of the best chain reactions in literature. And the prose is masterly: touches like the word "mournfully" indicate the narrator's detachment and his seemingly disinterested attempt simply to render the truth of things. It is elegant deadpan comic creation of a superb order.

Yet Kreisler is presented as much more than a farcical wildbody who collides with merry widows; he is also the ravager of Bertha Lunken, the murderer of Soltyk and finally of himself. Keisler's tragedy, Lewis argues, is empty and mechanical; but, without quibbling over what tragedy should mean, it seems doubtful that the word can accommodate itself to this usage without turning into little more than a synonym for "life." Clearly, we are meant to sympathize with Tarr's subsequent analysis of Kreisler as the failed artist who tries to get back into life, into sex, and finally into death. Furthermore, Lewis is concerned with this figure as an incarnation of the *Zeitgeist:* as a series of selves, each of which is related to that which precedes it in a strictly temporal manner. Thus, after the conquest of Bertha, Kreisler is presented at the window as a thing ". . . completely cut off from its raging self of the recent occurrence. It could do all these things: it appeared to be in a series of precipitate states: in this it resembled a switchback, rising slowly, in a steady innocent way, to the top of an incline, and then plunging suddenly down the other side with a catastrophic rush" (203).

Lewis suggested other tendencies (stormy pessimism, the romantic temperament), or all-too-human prototypes (Hitler and Goebbels) with which Kreisler was to be identified; but it is doubtful such an abstract exercise makes the book any more valid or interesting, or the "doing" of Kreisler himself more compelling. Recalling a remark quoted earlier about the crea-

tures of satire as "great intuitive figures of creation," we can say
(as with the case of Hobson) that what the figure *is* rather than
what it represents gives the only basis for judging the writer's
success in presentation. In creating Otto Kreisler, Lewis
builded better, dug deeper, than he or the confidently analytical Tarr quite knew.

For what Kreisler *is* fascinates and perplexes both Tarr and
Lewis. One of the strangest sequences in the novel consists of
Tarr's dogging of the German's footsteps and his leechlike at-
tachment to him evenings in the cafe, culminating in an unin-
vited visit to Kreisler's rooms that ends when Tarr is thrown
out. There is no clarity of motive, no evident purpose in Tarr's
actions; after he is turned out of Kreisler's rooms by a suddenly
produced dog whip, Tarr has the following uneasy meditation:

What really should he have done? He should, no doubt, having humorously instituted himself Kreisler's keeper, have humorously struggled
with him, when the idiot became obstreperous. But at that point his
humour had stopped. Then his humour had limitations?

Once and for all no one had a right to treat a man as he had Kreisler
and yet claim, when turned upon, immunity from action on the score
of the other's imbecility. In allowing the physical struggle any importance he allowed Kreisler an importance, too: this made his former
treatment of him unjustified.

(256)

Then, combining this experience with his Bertha Lunken
affair, Tarr is granted a moment of perception whose importance
goes beyond any mere filling-out or development of a character:

His sardonic dream of life got him, as a sort of quixotic dreamer of
inverse illusions, blows from the swift arms of windmills and attacks
from indignant and perplexed mankind. But he—unlike Quixote—
instead of having conceived the world as more chivalrous and marvellous than it was, had conceived it as emptied of all dignity, sense, and
generosity. *The drovers and publicans were angry at not being mistaken for a legendary chivalry, for knights and ladies!* The very wind-
mill resented not being taken for giants!—The curse of humour was in
him, anchoring him at one end of the see-saw whose movement and
contradiction was life.

(257)

The whole analysis of which these quotations are part is conducted with thoughtful rigor and candor; and, although it ends with a metaphysical statement of where Tarr is, the meditation is also moral, at times moralistic in tone. Tarr, like Lewis in a passage already quoted from *The Wild Body*, has committed himself to the role of metaphysical satirist who practices satire for its own sake since every person can be seen as imperfect, simply by his being a person instead of a work of art. The extraordinary thing about this passage from *Tarr* is the way in which that whole habit of mind is turned on, not in rejection, but in fuller understanding—with the recognition that the practice of such "humour," such satire, carries with it its own curse, and that it is faced in no trivial way by "life": by the gentle movement and contradiction of Bertha's pathetic objects as well as the violent Kreisler's dog whip.

Yet, as T. S. Eliot pointed out in his valuable *Egoist* review of the novel, Tarr is protected, all too well, by Lewis.[5] With the death of Kreisler, Tarr's affairs are wound up in a rather silly way: after a good deal of all-too-smartly-suggestive repartee with Anastasya (the section of the book is titled "Swagger Sex"), he throws up his hands and accepts life, marries Bertha Lunken to legitimize Kreisler's child while he dallies with the flashy Anastasya. Tarr is the perfect Shavian hero, but the comic resolution is too simple to provide a fully satisfactory ending. The "movement and contradiction" of life in the novel, as revealed in the career of Otto Kreisler, both resists the intellectual analysis Tarr gives it in the closing scenes and remains untouched by the "humour" that is the satirist's curse.

In this sense, the novel is not unified; but it would be pedantic to turn that fact into cause for lament; the stories in *The Wild Body* are unified only at the price of excluding certain complicated human and moral responses to experience which *Tarr* comes to terms with, at least partially. More importantly, Lewis' career as a literary artist and critic of society can be usefully inspected from the vantage point afforded by his first novel. Again and again the hero sallies forth, sometimes in the guise of Mr. Wyndham Lewis, often under other names and other guises, but always to do battle with life and always equipped with the curse of humor that makes art.

Behind the assorted forms of violence and imbecility dealt with
by the astonishing outpouring of Lewis' books in the late 1920's,
stands the figure of Kreisler. Although Tarr's windy diatribe with
Anastasya may seem pompous or inadequate since it follows
hard on the heels of Kreisler's suicide, it expresses the motive that
runs the deepest in the books to follow: " 'This is the essential
point to grasp: *Death* is the thing that differentiates art and life.
Art is identical with the idea of permanence. Art is a continuity
and not an individual spasm: but life is the idea of the person' "
(327). Kreisler, unlike Art, has no continuity, represents nothing;
it is finally for this reason that Tarr is, and Wyndham Lewis continued to be, obsessed by him.

CHAPTER 3

The End of Western Man: Lewis as Sage and Mocker

> Now, it is clear that the very absence of any powerful authority amongst us, and the prevalent doctrine of the duty and happiness of doing as one likes, and asserting our personal liberty, must tend to prevent the erection of any very strict standard of excellence, the belief in and very paramount authority of right reason, the recognition of our best self as anything very recondite and hard to come at.
>
> Arnold, *Culture and Anarchy*

> To build up a critical organism, composed of the most living material of observed fact, which could serve as an ally of new creative effort—something like an immense watch-dog trained to secure by its presence the fastness of the generally ill-protected theoretic man, guaranteed suitably to protect such minds as cared to avail themselves of it—that was the kind of thing I had in mind. . . .
>
> Lewis, *Time and Western Man*

THE most impressively productive years of Lewis' literary career—1926 through 1930—opened with the publication of *The Art of Being Ruled*, his most general and germinal critical work. In 1927 he published *The Lion and the Fox*, a study of Shakespeare and Machiavelli; revised and collected his short stories in *The Wild Body;* and produced his most important book of criticism, *Time and Western Man*. The same year, 1927, witnessed the first two numbers of his one-man periodical entitled *The Enemy*. Combining occasional sallies and forays into enemy camps and adorned by some of his most striking graphic designs, *The Enemy* acted as forcible advertisement for the writer's self.

45

Lewis was out to set everything straight, and he pursued this task with unwavering energy; whether the energy went into exposing the pretentions of Henri Bergson or into announcing that he, the real Wyndham Lewis, was not the same writer as D. B. Wyndham Lewis, another "satirist."

In 1928 he published the thoroughly revised *Tarr* and the first part of a longer work titled *The Childermass;* in 1929 came *Paleface* and the last *Enemy* pamphlet consisting mainly of an essay, "The Diabolical Principle." Finally with a huge crash in 1930 appeared *The Apes of God,* his monstrous demonstration of the Compleat Satirist at work. Producing eight books in five years is remarkable enough, but it should also be noted that none of them runs under three hundred pages and that four of them are very large productions indeed. Except for remarks suggesting the deadly seriousness with which he engaged in his task, the letters of these years reveal little of the motives behind this intense activity; but it is clear, at the very least, that the books were written out of profound dissatisfaction with postwar Western culture, particularly as it impinged on the artist.

Let us recall and imagine the situation of Wyndham Lewis the artist who in prewar London had enjoyed some reputation, even notoriety; had published a bold review; and had written a novel which was highly praised. His credentials as a creative artist established, he went off to be a gunner and did not die a heroic death for England; instead, he returned to experience—what? No dramatic event or personal crisis conveniently exists as a watershed. It has been customary, since Charles Handley-Read's chronology of Lewis' work, to refer to the years of the early 1920's as a "period of semi-retirement" [1] that lasted until it was romantically (and improbably) broken by the General Strike of 1926, at which point the aggressive man of letters sprang forth—the Enemy full-blown.

This romantic biography was probably encouraged by Lewis himself, always ready (as in the titles chosen for his magazines—*Blast* and *The Enemy*) to give the public a bit of sensational matter. A less dramatic explanation would be to note that, when the war ended, Lewis at thirty-six possessed a reputation which could well have been exploited in the interests of a fashionable career as a graphic artist, with perhaps a gossipy novel produced every so often for good-measured variety. What happened instead was that he became a sociologist-diagnostician of Western culture. Finding that the activity of being a painter or a novelist—a specialist in one medium—did not permit him to express certain kinds of understanding and mastery of society, he adopted a prose medium that suited his ends. Lewis would be the first to admit that there is no place for combativeness and controversy in a work of art, and in *Rude Assignment* he claims that he has no particular fondness for controversy. But the political, sociological, and literary forces that dominated the postwar world of the 1920's had to be combated and if possible defeated so that there would be time to write novels and paint pictures. We shall see, particularly with regard to *Time and Western Man,* how astonishingly creative Lewis makes the combat.

The section from T. S. Eliot's letter quoted earlier mildly criticized Lewis for trying to write eight or ten books at a time rather than concentrating his energies. In fact, the letters of the early 1920's reveal that many of the books which appeared later were offshoots of one projected great work. Several mentions are made in 1923–24 of a book *The Man of the World* which Lewis says is taking longer to write than he had originally anticipated. In 1925 he states that he has sent the Macmillan publishing house a primarily philosophical work called *The Politics of the Personality* which, if accepted, was to be followed by one more political in concern, *The Politics of Philistia.* The latter book (also referred to as *The Politics of the Primitive* and *Critique of Class*) became *The Art of Being Ruled* (1926), and the former, *Time and Western Man* (1927).

Together, the two central books run to almost a thousand pages; and, as might perhaps be expected from even a small knowledge of the circumstances of their composition and publication, there is some overlapping (and also with *The Lion and the Fox*). That fact never seemed to bother Lewis in the least; he continued to quote passages of material from *The Art of Being Ruled* in his later books, just in case, as was likely, the reader didn't remember or didn't have the particular book at hand. Even with this overlapping of concern and closeness of composition the two books are quite different in their effect. One can begin by stating that, although the philosophical section of *Time and Western Man* is overlong, the book as a whole is much easier to read through continuously than is *The Art of Being Ruled* and that

this fact is due not simply to technical differences in organization
of material but, more importantly, to the manner Lewis adopts
toward his material—differences that will emerge later on as we
consider each book separately. But they have in common at least
one important antecedent: Matthew Arnold's *Culture and
Anarchy*.

Each section of *The Art of Being Ruled* is introduced by quotations taken more often from Arnold than from any other writer;
and there are many ways in which the emerging shape of Lewis'
career brings to mind his predecessor's. Arnold's first volume of
poetry was published in 1849 when he was twenty-seven; *Culture
and Anarchy*, from which Lewis takes all his quotations, ran as a
series of articles in *The Cornhill Magazine* in 1867–68; Lewis published his first fiction in 1909 also at age twenty-seven and *The Art
of Being Ruled* appears seventeen years later. Both writers in their
mid-forties, having attained some success in the arts (though certainly Lewis' life was less public and distinguished than Arnold's), looked upon a world in which the future of art was, to say
the least, insecure; in which the coarsening and brutalization of
taste proceeded apace; in which freedom was equated with "doing
as one likes"; and in which the cheapest kind of revolutionary
sensation prevailed as long as it was sufficiently novel and mechanical. Objective standards of beauty, repose, or sanity were
rendered meaningless while the word "classical" became synony-
mous with "reactionary" or "outmoded."

Arnold and Lewis are very clear that it was nothing less than
the *Zeitgeist* with which they were struggling; and, though each of
them was committed to reason as an ideal value, they were not so
utopian as to suppose that their prose would prevail simply
through its own sweet reasonableness. Lewis went to much
greater lengths of stylistic excess and polemical outrageousness
than did Arnold, but the important point of similarity lies in the
adoption by each of an ironic and satiric relation to his opponents.

Both writers lacked the specialist training in certain disciplines
—philosophy, economics, physics—which the endeavors they
undertook seemingly demanded. The only answer to the cautious
man who would adduce these lacks as grounds for skepticism is to
show him the books at issue and let him then say how these deficiencies manifest themselves; and Lewis faced up to such a criticism with a fine excess in the preface to Book I of *Time and*

Western Man by saying: "I do not feel impelled to explain myself when I am examining a mere philosopher: he speaks my language, usually with less skill, but otherwise much the same as I do" (10). Both Arnold and Lewis have been chastised for the incorrigibly loose way they conduct their arguments. Mr. Eliot, for example, registered his dismay at Arnold's use of language[2] (the "application" of ideas to life); while, in speaking of Lewis' polemics, it has become commonplace to talk as if his pretense at conducting an argument is merely a bluff when in reality words are being used as heavy weapons of assault to bludgeon and overwhelm the reader.[3] Yet it is not usual for the critic who accuses Lewis of practicing a sham on his readers to demonstrate painstakingly just how and where some argument is really fraudulent; thus the accusation turns into an irresponsibly high-handed way of avoiding taking issue with any specific argument.

Lewis' affinity with Arnold, the fact that it is possible to feel some continuity of tradition between them, can be carried only so far; no one would look, for instance, for Arnold's urbane self-deprecating charm in Lewis' more vigorous onslaughts. But the comparison suggests a larger way of understanding the nature of Lewis' manner toward his subject and audience, particularly in the critical books of the 1920's. In an appreciation of Lewis' achievement, Walter Allen adduces an extremely apposite paragraph from John Holloway's book *The Victorian Sage*. Holloway is speaking of Carlyle: "Through Carlyle's prose the nerve of proof—in the readily understood and familiar sense of straightforward argument—simply cannot be traced; and the succession of arbitrary and unproved assertions tends to forfeit our attention. Yet this is only a subordinate difficulty, because although proof is clearly missing, it is by no means clear what would supply this lack, as it is by no means clear what needs proof."

And Holloway describes the situation of the "sage" in general as follows: "He does not and probably cannot rely on logical and formal argument alone or even at all. His main task is to quicken his reader's perceptiveness and he does this by making a far wider appeal than the exclusively rational appeal. He draws upon resources cognate, at least, with those of the artist in words." [4] Our concern with Lewis as a sage is to describe some of the ways his books accomplish their imaginative assault on the reader and quicken his perceptiveness.

I   The Art of Being Ruled

Probably the three events that figure most significantly as background to Lewis' first major critical book are World War I, the Russian revolution and establishment of a Leninist "dictatorship" (and Lewis called it that in 1926), and the rise to power of Italian Fascism. In such a world all serious politics had to be revolutionary politics—whether of the Left or of the Right; for Lewis sees Fascism as but a faction of the extreme Left that had burst through to the other side. In the middle of nowhere stood the liberalist democracies of Western Europe and America in post-Arnoldian anarchy. What anarchy means for Lewis is primarily fragmentation, a sense of the self as discontinuous and of life in pieces. As does the individual man, so Western Europe reflects this same piecemeal enfeebled unreality without organization or vitality.

If *The Waste Land* comes to mind, it is because Lewis' voice in *The Art of Being Ruled* is as disillusioned and at times as grim as the prophetic shorer of fragments in Eliot's poem. But to be without illusions does not necessitate mere passive supplication; man had better shore some fragments, since there is nothing particularly attractive about suffering death by water. Early in the book the following warning occurs: "In such a fluid world we should by all rights be building boats rather than houses. But this essay is a sort of ark, or dwelling for the mind, designed to float and navigate; and we should all be wise, with or without covenants, to provide ourselves with some such shell in everything, rather than to rely on any conservative structures. For a very complete and profound inundation is at hand. After *us* comes the Deluge: more probably than not, however, before that, and out of its epigrammatic sequence" (16).

To speak, therefore, of the book's apocalyptic character is not fanciful; but at certain times, fortunately, Lewis forgets about the Deluge to come. In the main, though, his person in *The Art of Being Ruled* is that of a sterner Tarr, one who hopes to wipe the English grin from as many faces as possible. Even the satirist's own "curse of humour"—something much more useful and admirable than the English grin—is largely held in abeyance, at least in comparison to Lewis' other books. Instead, the analysis churns along at a stiff, often heavy-handed, stop-and-start pace; fre-

quently the author replaces one topic with another in the most
abrupt and confusing manner. It takes a very well-equipped
reader indeed to move with confidence from the end of one chapter to the beginning of the next one; for example, four chapter
titles from the second part of the book, headed "Agricultural
Thought and Industrial Thought," read

    I.   "Bolshevism and the West"
   II.   Different solutions of the problem of the Yahoo
  III.   Violence and "kindliness"; Mr. Bernard Shaw and
                                         Mr. Bertrand Russell
  IV.   Vegetarianism and capital punishment

These titles look discontinuous, and the text often seems so as we
read; but a main point of the book is to encourage a reader who is
not a machine to make relations and connections between aspects
of modern social and political experience that seem unrelated or
merely contiguous. As an apocalyptic book, it has to be about
everything since the world as a whole is going to be flooded. *The
Art of Being Ruled* is difficult to read in part because it has a subject but no theme—or rather so many themes that their relation to
one another is often puzzling.

Nevertheless, the main outlines are clear enough. Lewis sets
himself no less a task than to analyze the causes of European decay. He finds them to lie in a commitment to "freedom"—to the
word, not the fact—rather than to a strongly centralized community governed, it might well be, by despotic authority. He is
extremely respectful toward, if a trifle appalled by, the two
authoritarian systems that could then be observed in Europe; unfortunately, his interest in unmasking and ridiculing the remaining shams of liberalist-democratic thought makes him all too
ready to ignore or to whitewash the liabilities of non-democratic
systems. This blindness was to be Lewis' great limitation as a political analyst throughout his career; even as he looks back on that
career in *Rude Assignment,* he speaks as if his main mistake had
been to care too much about something that was already dead—
Western civilization. But surely this allegiance is not so difficult
for us to accept; some still find it possible, even in this heyday of
non-Western culture, to save some piety for Western man.

What *is* most troubling can be seen in the gap between the

matters Lewis is analyzing—often in exceedingly complex and
suggestive ways—and the simplicity of his recommendations (if
they are such, for he is not always clear) for improved conditions.
These recommendations can virtually be reduced to the assertion
that, using Goethe's terms, all men are either "puppets" or
"natures." The puppets *really* want to submit to and obey the "natures"; the cant of democracy provides them, however, with inappropriate notions of personal "freedom" and, as regards the community, costly ones of irresponsible doing-as-one-likes. Since, in
fact, there is no comparison possible between a "puppet" and a
"nature," no "puppet" should feel abused by or inferior to his better. The true revolutionary, as opposed to the common vulgarizer
of revolutionary sentiment, insists on the promotion—exactly *how*
Lewis does not indicate, but we can imagine some ways—of this
distinction. False or fashonable revolutionaries encourage men to
better themselves, or to express their personalities, when they
have nothing except a group personality to express. If a true revolutionary, however,

. . . you will find many curious paradoxes in your relation both with
the fashionable life of the wealthy amateur of the millionnaire world,
and with the revolutionary popularizer. A prophecy of a civilization
that will emerge from the present ruin will be present to you in the
work of a few inventive men of letters, science, and art. . . . But a
deadweight of organized optimism will press on your chest. Everything will conspire to bully or hypnotize you into a *best of all* possible
worlds attitude. You will have to be a very irreconcilable individual
not to find yourself on this much too-obviously 'winning side.'

(153–54)

This "very irreconcilable individual," the true revolutionary, is,
of course, none other than Wyndham Lewis' best self: denying the
group-rhythms of herd-revolutionaries, he sees through and exposes the optimistic shams of liberalist progress. Yet in the section
of the book entitled "Fascism as an Alternative," the "irreconcilable individual" with a sudden gesture of weary annoyance shows
himself not so irreconcilable after all as he speaks of "some modified form of Fascism" as probably the best kind of Socialism for
Anglo-Saxon countries. The proposed ingredients of this mixture
—a dash of "sovietic proletarian sentiment" and "as little coercion
as is compatible with good sense"—are vaguer and less revealing

than the sentence which closes the paragraph: "In short, to get some sort of peace to enable us to work, we should naturally seek the most powerful and stable authority that can be devised" (369–70). The referent of "us" is not specified, but it surely points to "natures" rather than "puppets" and perhaps most especially to artists like Wyndham Lewis. At any rate, there follows a glowing account of Mussolini's reforms and the disappearance, much to Lewis' pleasure, of democratic-liberalist politics in Italy. In such a passage, coming as an emphatic summarizing spot in the book, the "deadweight of organized optimism" has pressed on the writer's chest; and he has become reconciled to it, even to the extent of saluting this "too-obviously winning side." [5]

The most satisfactory, and in Lewis' own terms, truly revolutionary sections of *The Art of Being Ruled* are those in which he stays clear of any programmatic activities and analyzes the manners of contemporary culture. For example, large sections of the book are devoted to what might be called an expanded exploration of Henry James's perception (from which sprang *The Bostonians*) of a decline in the sentiment of sex in America. James was also looking at a society that had recently emerged from war; Lewis sees the "sex-war" as a fashionable revolutionary attack upon outmoded institutions such as the family and heterosexuality. The feminist revolution comes appropriately at a time when men are sick of fighting wars—in other words, of being men—and so, as Lewis puts it, "The homo is the legitimate child of the suffragette." Some of the livelier parts of the book deal with the phenomenon of the "transformed man" or *shaman,* and a good deal of anthropological evidence is produced, without evident irony, that there were indeed *shamans* in eastern Siberia from whose example we are invited to argue back to our own society.

Lewis is making a serious point in relating feminism, postwar sexual inversion, and the cults of being-a-child and being-an-artist to a larger war declared in the name of sensation against the intellect in all its forms. Yet the number of pages and amount of energy so enthusiastically devoted to this discussion should be a warning that much of the interest it holds is a function of its satiric and imaginative life, rather than in anything it may "prove" about what was really the case in 1926. That is, while we may cast our eyes over page after page telling us how the new male wants to be a female, the invert a child, and everyone a certified artist, the

argument comes alive when a particular figure is suddenly created
who embodies these abstractions. We are told, for example, that
there is a great war on the part of sensation against the intellect
and that many phenomena are aspects of this war; abruptly the
phenomena coalesce in the figure of a writer:

> Proust himself is an arch sex-mixer, a great democrat, a great enemy
> of the intellect. For he desires in the deepest way to see everything
> converted into terms of sex, to have everything and everybody on that
> violent, scented, cloying and unreal plane, where there is nothing that
> cannot be handled, the very substance of illusion sniffed at and tasted
> by everybody, and put to the uses of sensation. In that world most of
> the values of the intellect are reversed. . . . No man is a hero to his
> valet: and it is to a world of highly energized, orthodoxly perverted
> valets, with a great many scores to pay off, that Proust invites society.
> In this sense he is a great revolutionary figure.
>
> (275–76)

No matter how distasteful Lewis finds the work of this "figure,"
and his remarks about Proust are often insensitively doctrinaire,
he does not shirk the task of creating Proust, the arch sex-mixer.
Lewis' satiric imagination is, characteristically for the creator of
Kreisler or Tarr, engaged in dramatizing metaphorically a figure
in a world, rather than in debunking or reducing some static entity whom everyone knows as "Proust." To describe Proust's world
in 1926 or today as one of "orthodoxly perverted valets with a
good many scores to pay off" takes one brilliantly in imagination
to the borders of that world. It is a report on Proust by a strong
mind expressing itself in an elegantly harsh style; and, like the
book from which it is taken, it must be felt primarily as just that—
not as a proposition to be agreed or disagreed with.

If this approach to the book seems excessively literary or even
evasive, it is no more so than that of the author's when he nears
the realm of apocalypse he himself has prophesied. After us the
deluge, well and good; but exactly where does the prophet stand
in relation to it? On the one hand, Lewis is the artist, committed
to the outside of things in all their specific differences; he is that
maintainer and proclaimer of differentiation who saves us from
romantic merger and destruction. Yet the great figures of the
book, true revolutionaries such as Proust or Proudhon or Péguy
who look on the world with completely unillusioned eyes, heroi-

cally consign the world away. Lewis quotes Péguy and comments
as follows: " '*Tout le monde est malheureux dans le monde mod-
erne*', the climax of his despairing rhetoric has the true hebraic
note of boundless pessimism. And all these ardent, intoxicated,
eloquent men desire the destruction of the world, in a sort of restless, but virtuous, impotence" (323). The tribute is handsomely
put. At the same time, it leaves us curious as to how Lewis will
come to terms with his own ardent eloquence.

II   *Emergence of* The Enemy

Lewis was certainly unwilling in 1927 to see himself as a prophet
of destruction crying out on life with restless, if virtuous, impotence. The difference between *The Art of Being Ruled* and the
first two issues of his magazine *The Enemy* that appeared in Feb-
ruary and October of the next year, might be compared to that
between a guidebook to the territory and what Lewis at one point
refers to as particular "mining and sapping operations" calculated
to make the territory freer of malign influences. The motto for the
magazine was taken from Plutarch's *Moralia* and read in part as
follows: "Thine enemy, as thou knowest well enough, watcheth
continually, spying and prying into all thine actions. As for our
friends, it chanceth many times that they fall extreme sick, yes,
and die while we defer and put off from day to day to go and visit
them, or make small reckoning of them: but as touching our enemies we are so observant, we curiously inquire even after their
very dreams."

The not-so-gentle art with which Lewis made enemies was,
therefore, necessarily different from the procedure of a guidebook. Although he proudly maintained that many people found
The Art of Being Ruled offensive, it was nevertheless a relatively
detached and philosophical argument compared to the direct
goading of *The Enemy*. And, although many names were named
in the guidebook and called to account for positions they had
taken, there was as yet a relatively small backlog of feuds and
recriminations to summon up. These developed mightily as Lewis
went along, for the *Enemy* pamphlets not only name names and
call them to account, they also *call* names—and make it exceedingly clear that the voice which calls them is neither detached in
manner nor impersonal in its condemnations.

We shall see later on how concerned Lewis is in *The Lion and*

the Fox, also published in 1927, to combat the notion of Shakespeare's (or any great writer's) supposed "impersonality." Lewis'
own situation is closer to Pope's in the *Epilogue to the Satires* in
which the poet is urged by his friend to cease naming names—especially powerful ones—and to be content with speaking out
mildly and impersonally against vices in the abstract. The destruction of this argument and a vindication of personal interest speaking in the name of a wider public good is the poem's subject.
Lewis' campaigns in *The Enemy* against the "time-school" writers,
primitivist art, and the "super-realism" of the *Transition* group are
of course carried on in the interests of truth and the public benefit
that will accrue from its being published. But there is no doubt in
evidence from the letters and from the many personal notes in the
writings under consideration that his criticism, like Eliot's, was an
attempt to clear the way for understanding and acceptance of his
own unfashionable artistry. The large difference is that Lewis, like
Pound (and in Pound's own phrase about himself), threw rocks
through the front windows and left Eliot free to steal in the back
door and make off with the swag.

Throwing rocks takes many forms in *The Enemy,* depending
upon how much ammunition is needed to destroy the particular
shop front in question. The larger operations were later incorporated in *Time and Western Man* and in *Paleface,* but there are
many minor demolition jobs which illustrate the particular kind of
satirical weapons developed in *Enemy* campaigns and never
wholly relinquished afterwards. Perhaps the best of these jobs is
the second editorial note from *The Enemy* #2, devoted to a report on the then recent popular success of Kathryn Mayo's
Mother India. Lewis begins calmly by announcing that the book
breaks a depth record by sinking to a new level of vulgar untruth,
and he congratulates Miss Mayo on managing to insult three hundred million people. He then takes up the book's argument that,
due to certain premature sex practices, the inhabitants of India
are, unlike us, "degenerate."

The source of Miss Mayo's steamy statistics seems to be a book
by the Abbé Dubois on Hindu manners; Lewis, who quotes Dr.
Max Muller to the effect that the Abbé died in 1848, suggests that
Miss Mayo's use of such evidence as an indicator of present Indian *moeurs* is ingenuous to say the least. Then, taking the absurd

title of the book, he imagines possibilities for a *Mother America* to be written by an Indian lady visitor to the United States:

The indian lady visitor to the United States, let us suppose, has arrived. She "courteously" requests to be "shown over," and in her book she can say how very "courteous," at least (that looks well, it shows how fair and unbiased you are), everybody was (how very *stupidly* courteous to such a person she may privately reflect): and she could (very easily) have a remarkably "highly-placed diplomatist" or "a great inventor" perhaps (that would look well) always at her elbow, just as Miss Mayo always has a *particularly* "high-caste Brahmin" at her elbow to inform against *other* high-caste Brahmins: the indian lady visitor or inquisitor, the "restless analyst" from the East, could quote extensively from some american equivalent of the *Loom of Youth*, and tell the horrified Indian Public how in all the schools and universities of the United States homosexuality was rampant: then she could tell the usual stories of pregnant high-school girls—reveal whole classes carried away in one brake to the Lying-in-Hospital: she could state *as a fact* that all american men were sexually impotent at thirty (hence the Broadway girl-shows), and that self-abuse was intense and universal throughout the 48 states of the Union: she could describe the death-rate per day in an American city by violent crime, quote Mencken for bits about the monstrosities of Prohibition: and she could wind up by saying that America is a "physical menace" (cf. p. 23 *Mother India*) to the Hindu.

(xix)

Warming to the task, Lewis imagines other successively funnier ways the book could be written; and he caps his analysis by suggesting William Prescott's *Conquest of Mexico* as an appropriate source for evidence about contemporary American blood sacrifices. The title of the imaginary book would perhaps be *Hail Columbia, Happy Land.*

If this is harsh treatment for a lady's book, it at least destroyed her work on its own terms by energetically weaving them into a coarse sex comedy that exposes the limitations of Miss Mayo as a restless analyst of other cultures. And if, as it turns out, Alec Waugh's current best-seller *The Loom of Youth* can be pilloried at the same time, so much the better; for one of Lewis' main themes from *The Art of Being Ruled* onwards is the interrelatedness of sex and politics. The passage quoted above is Matthew Arnold

without the good taste; Lewis' deference to "Miss Mayo" fits in-
aptly and hilariously with the gross fantasies foisted on her by
analogy. But with the important exception of this tall tale, the
method of damning quotation, the adducing of related instances
of vulgar absurdity (Waugh's novel), and the deep sense of contempt and disgust for this product of anarchy, all mark the Arnoldian heritage.

In a final sentence about *Mother India* Lewis says, "It promotes
that excellent feeling of brotherly love between nations and races
that is so very useful and comfortable for all of us," which shows
that he, like Arnold (and Swift too), can lapse on occasions into a
heavy sarcasm. Such manners would not do in *The Criterion,* even
though Eliot might have agreed with Lewis' viewpoint on the
book. *The Enemy's* success in any particular foray is dependent in
large part on the comic life of the show he produces. In a letter
replying to Arnold Bennett's charge that such loud contentious-
ness was to be deplored, Lewis concluded by predicting that with
the resuscitation of the word "enemy" and its use in social relations "society would immediately assume much more definite and
interesting patterns. There would be a bold arabesque of black
and white, in place of the present undescriptive mauve or sickly
heliotrope" (167). The handsome designs which make up the cov-
ers of these magazines admirably lay down some of the patterns;
they are fitted to the boldness and vigorous life of the whole one-
man experiment.

III   Time and Western Man

Twenty years after the publication of *Time and Western
Man,* Lewis picturesquely referred to it in *Rude Assignment* as
"a substantial fortress, once full of vigorous defenders, but now
silent, probably a place where bats hang upside down and jackals
find a musty bedchamber" (192). By the late 1940's, cosmic instead of Western man claimed his allegiance; but Lewis never
repudiated the substance of the book, only what it was constructed to defend—an entity now no longer there, if it ever had
been. His particular criticism of the "time-mind," or "time-
philosophy," as it expressed itself in literature, popular culture,
and the systems of ideas standing behind them, remained as valid
as ever. "In that bleak fortress there is still much loot," Lewis

added in retrospect; and he was right. The sense of excited discovery a reader feels upon encountering the book for the first time
is as strong today as it was for Yeats in 1927.[6]

For Lewis, the "time-mind" is the twentieth-century mind,
spellbound before "the flux." Imaginative and expository works are
alike engaged in redefining "reality" as wholly temporal; in turning the self into a packet of selves, endlessly replacing one another; and in translating all spatial "physical" characteristics into
temporal "mental" ones. That such a broad attack sounds simplified and over-schematic is doubtless true. Lewis put the case
against himself with good grace by admitting to a seeming nar-
rowness of position and illiberality of spirit, qualities he saw as
essential to the success of his polemic. Hopefully, illiberality and
overstatement would lead to an awareness of the unconscious assumptions on which the works of the "time-mind" are founded. In
this sense his task was analogous to that of R. G. Collingwood's
ideal metaphysician whose work was to bring to light the presup-
positions on which other philosophers construct their systems.[7]

The first part of *Time and Western Man* is titled "The Revolutionary Simpleton" and appeared as the bulk of *The Enemy* #1.
Most of this section is comprised of chapters on Pound and a long
"Analysis of the Mind of James Joyce"; it will be dealt with when
we discuss Lewis' attitudes toward his literary contemporaries. For
the moment, we are concerned with the more directly philosophical second part that is four times as long and consists of a critical
examination of the time-school philosophers: in particular of
Bergson, Alfred North Whitehead, and Samuel Alexander, but
with glances at William James and Bertrand Russell. An overlong
but devastating attack on Spengler's "chronological philosophy"
follows; finally Lewis makes an excursion into the history of ideas
for purposes of tracing the fortunes of "the subject" and "the object" with a view toward rehabilitating them, or at least of suggesting their roles in the writer's own epistemology and metaphysics. Taken as a whole, the philosophical criticism seems
worthy of more serious consideration than it has had by any historian of ideas engaged in describing the philosophic situation in
the first twenty years of this century. Although such a description
is not attempted here, it should be possible and instructive to follow the criticism Lewis makes of *one* of these philosophers in

order to show how that philosopher's position is dramatized, exposed, and then rejected by the critic whose own position is quite different.

In these terms the treatment of Whitehead is fuller and more revealing than that of Bergson, since Lewis sees the latter as the demon behind everything; Bergson drags us into the flux of sensation, is scornful of attempts to use language and logic in the service of valuable precise utterance, and is given to the "poetic" style William James so much admired but that Lewis refers to with contempt as "saying it with flowers." Early in the second part of the book Lewis contrasts the characters of Whitehead and Bergson by claiming that, while the former is at least an *"honest* sentimentalist of the 'radical' english-schoolmaster type," the latter "is the perfect philosophical ruffian of the darkest and most forbidding description: and he pulls every emotional lever on which he can lay his hands" (174). In fact, Lewis is so temperamentally the opposite of Bergson that his criticism loses some of the authority it might have in contrast, say, with the cooler but no less adverse treatments of the philosopher by George Santayana and Bertrand Russell.[8]

With Whitehead the case is quite different. *Science and the Modern World* appeared in 1925, was favorably received, and, then as now, had been largely unsubjected to rigorous scrutiny. The Whitehead that Lewis criticizes is wholly the philosopher of one book; but since, particularly for students of literature, *Science and the Modern World* has taken on such important authority, becoming at times a sanctified home for quotations of assurance that poetry does matter, we should try to understand the point of Lewis' patronizing evocation of "this honest sentimentalist."

He begins the attack by announcing that Whitehead, like Bergson, finds inadequate the spatializing habits of common sense whereby a particular object is located in a particular place. Since Bergson has taught us to "take time seriously" (in Alexander's phrase), there is no need to shackle ourselves to outmoded spatializing habits, nor to the tenets of a materialistic science and its attendant doctrines of an external world of dead matter, devoid of qualities or purposes. In place of this world, Whitehead proposes a new one of "events" or "prehensive unifications" that are neither simply mind nor matter and that occur at a sudden realization of space-time. It was only what Whitehead terms "The Fallacy of

Misplaced Concreteness" which led scientists and philosophers to
assume that the external world consisted of dead colorless matter.
The Romantic poets, especially Shelley and Wordsworth, are
praised for their vivid protests against such a world and for their
pantheistic impulses of identification with the aspects of nature
around them. Since concrete fact is process, in a sense everything
is involved in everything else: we live in a world that is real, that
is alive and that demands a philosophy adequate to its vitality.
The name Whitehead gives to his attempt to provide one is "organic mechanism."

Lewis' main objection to Whitehead's scheme is that, while it
advertises itself as the supporter of life and announces that we
need no longer believe in a materialistic universe, it is in fact
much more insidiously mechanical, therefore much more abstract,
and therefore more unreal than the world picture it sets out to
depose. Put in terms of any advantages man derives from this
replacement of dead matter by organism, the benefits are meager;
after all, says Lewis, *we* were organic all along, but now our chairs
and tables as well must participate in a common world of organic
"events." On the other hand, the loss is considerable: the invitation to merge with the new-live world about us means that our
substantial self is traded in for a series of selves created anew with
each "event." And, as the substantial self disappears, so does the
world—the objection is importantly an esthetic one: "By this proposed transfer from the beautiful *objective, material* world of
common-sense, over to the 'organic' world of chronological men-
talism, you lose not only the clearness of outline, the static beauty
of the things you commonly apprehend; you lose also the clearness of outline of your own individuality which apprehends them"
(175).

Lest this criticism be disregarded as merely the sort that a certain kind of plastic artist might make, Lewis goes on to use Whitehead's own terms against him. Whitehead sees philosophy as the
critic of abstractions and his own particular task to be that of
criticizing the needless and perverse ones dominant in science and
philosophy since the seventeenth century. Lewis seizes upon the
argument to make the point that what Whitehead would substi-
tute for them—a world of organic mechanism, "prehensive" unifications, "eternal objects" (such as color, which in Whitehead's
language "haunts time like a spirit")—is in fact more abstract

than the scheme it would replace. The following passage shows Lewis at the task of associating Whitehead's language with certain aspects of the time-philosophy:

In place of the characteristic static "form" of greek Philosophy, you have a series, a group, or, as Professor Whitehead says, a *reiteration*. In place of a "form" you have a "formation"—as it is characteristically called—a repetition of a particular shape; you have a battalion of forms in place of one form. In your turn, "you" become the series of your temporal repetitions; you are no longer a centralized self, but a spun-out, strung-along series, a pattern-of-a-self, depending like the musical composition upon time; an *object*, too, always in the making, who *are* your states. So you are a *history:* there must be no Present for you. You are an historical object, since your mental or time-life has been as it were objectified. The valuable advantages of being a "subject," will perhaps scarcely be understood by the race of *historical objects* that may be expected to ensue.

(181)

The analysis begins with Whitehead but quickly broadens to something that might be regarded as the time-philosopher's ideal man. One of the dangers or limitations of such argument is that, in its eagerness to describe and excoriate a system of ideas, it makes an individual philosopher more typical, more representative than he need be; thus "Whitehead" often means something less than the student of his works might desire. It is also true that Lewis' contempt for Whitehead's vocabulary is in part attributable to his own lack of interest in post-Newtonian physics. Lewis is perfectly happy with the existence of two cultures, and approves of the scientists getting on with their work as long as the claims of art (and of philosophy) are not dictated to. Whitehead's attempt to put the cultures together, as it were, is precisely what Lewis does not want to have succeed.[9] No doubt he was fighting a losing battle, but it was well worth fighting, especially since his position is not dictated by motives of a sentimentally esthetic fussiness or by a distaste for cold, cruel science.

Lewis is not insisting that the artist's world of concrete common-sense objects is superior or preferable to the scientist's world of "scientific objects." But, as we have indicated, he resists the humane philosopher-scientist who would unite the worlds. Dr. Whitehead is "all for the poets and artists," yet poets and artists can do very well without the kind of support that attempts to "reinstate" the art object with an up-to-date philosophic vocabulary. Part of what Lewis objects to is the historical sentimentality Whitehead displays when he looks back and sees a poet ill-at-ease in the old dispensation. Tennyson is the example: Whitehead quotes the line from *In Memoriam*—"The stars, she whispers, 'blindly' run"—and goes on to assert rather crudely that either they blindly run or they do not, as if Tennyson's language could *really* work itself out in the world. Lewis does not mention this lapse but lands instead on Whitehead's public comforting of Tennyson as a distracted spirit attempting to come to terms with materialistic science:

Tennyson is for ever consoled by being assured that, although it is true that the molecule *blindly runs* (as he put it), nevertheless it *runs according to a pattern.* (For instance: "The electron blindly runs either within or without the body; but it runs within the body in accordance with its character within the body; that is to say, in accordance with the original plan of the body, and this plan includes the mental state." The body and mind, in their turn, run blindly, too, within a still larger organism, and so on. This may be true; but it is difficult to see how it is cheerful.)

(182–83)

The comfort that this resolution of Tennyson's problem offers is a cold one indeed: "So the molecule is still a blind mouse in the same way as a gigantic mouse which is its pattern. Happy little mouse! And (after hearing this) happy-ever-afterwards would, of course, Lord Tennyson be, if this good news could reach him. Or so Professor Whitehead thinks, . . ." (183). If this statement is sneering, Lewis has made the most of it by indulging himself only after he has made a cogent objection to Whitehead's Olympian correction of poor Tennyson. As for just how Lewis' own treatment of Tennyson might differ from Whitehead's, we can only speculate; it is probable that, rather than helping out Tennyson with his problem in the manner of a "radical" English schoolmaster, Lewis would incline more towards the generally shared "hard" attitude of Verlaine, Yeats, and Eliot toward the poet— that his business was not to have deep thoughts about purpose in the cosmos but to exercise his superb ear and sensuous capacities of language.

In fact, although he never fully states it, the pious solemnity

attendant upon "taking time seriously" is what Lewis finds distasteful. The sharp *reductio ad absurdum* of his irony is seen at its
best in *Time and Western Man*, perhaps because the principal
philosophers he criticizes seem devoid of anything approaching
irony. In this connection it is revealing that Lewis expresses admiration for Berkeley and G. E. Moore and that he admits that, of
all the time-philosophers, he is most in sympathy with William
James, finding him "philosophically the best of company" (257),
even though he disapproves of his underlying principles.

The culminating moment in this criticism of Whitehead occurs
when Lewis quotes the most famous passage in *Science and the
Modern World* that begins with a picture of nature as seen by the
materialistic scientific-philosopher—"a dull affair, soundless,
scentless, colourless; merely the hurrying of material, endlessly,
meaninglessly." Whitehead praises this science for its genius of
efficiency, admits that it is still reigning without a rival, and then
with a flourish says that the concept is "quite unbelievable": "This
conception of the universe is surely framed in terms of high abstractions, and the paradox only arises because we have mistaken
our abstractions for concrete realities."

Who is the mistaken "we," Lewis asks; and he concludes that
perhaps Whitehead is really talking about himself. The artist's
and poet's world was never the dull affair that is described; therefore Whitehead's praise of Shelley and Wordsworth for insisting
that it was *not* a dull affair is irrelevant and misleading. Although
Lewis does not criticize Whiteheads' pocket history of English
poetry, he might have done so by asking whether any readable
eighteenth-century poet between Pope and Wordsworth saw nature in the terms that so appall Whitehead. And why, Lewis argues, should not the scientist work on with his dull and drab
world that doubtless is not so to him; let his picture of the world
be "quite unbelievable" as long as it continues to be useful for his
purposes.

More generally, Lewis' philosophical convictions oppose any attempts to break down the dualism of mind and nature by uniting
them in "events," "time," "pure experience," or whatever neutral
term can be mustered up, whether the unifier is Whitehead or
Bergson or William James. Walter Allen has called attention to the
Cartesian bent of Lewis' mind; it is seen at its most forceful in the
book under discussion as that mind spurns the invitation to heal

the split between itself and nature that had been in evidence since the day, in Yeats's colorful phrase, when Descartes decided he could think better in his bed than out of it. Lewis' rejection of such an invitation is a matter of conviction rather than whimsy or perversity; for this unity would involve compromise: a giving-up of the self's strong identity in favor of a more egalitarian togetherness. The argument against Whitehead and the time-philosophers is basically that the "togetherness" in a world of flux, which they are determined to take seriously, is inimical to both scientist and artist alike—not to mention the "puppets" organized under time-propaganda.

On the other hand, by insisting on our apartness from nature, the primary values of individuality and artistic differentiation are recognized; nature, the external world, should be kept as dead as possible so that our own life may appear more real to us. Lewis concludes his main criticism of Whitehead by suggesting that, if philosophers are bent on handing the "secondary" qualities—color, light, sound—back to nature (though the poet knows nothing of these distinctions among kinds of qualities), we should insist that deadness, or immobility, receive its rightful place among the rest. Surely, he insists with rhetorical sweep, our primary impression of the external world is its stability—there are those lumpish chairs and tables that surround us. If everything sensationally perceived is to be called "real," the deadness of nature is as real as any other quality it may possess. And he concludes: "It is merely the enlightened materialism of Whitehead that makes him so eager to banish it, and to put a nervous tic into the limbs of the statue, or prove to us that all poets have been pantheists" (212).

This survey of Lewis' criticism of Whitehead is selective; our treatment of the four-hundred-odd pages that make up Part Two of *Time and Western Man* has been selective indeed. The attempt has been to suggest, by quotation and exposition from a representative section of that book, what its overall character is like. Perhaps Lewis would not object to this procedure since he himself instituted and christened "The Taxi-Cab Drive Test for Fiction," which is performed by inferring the quality of a whole novel from the quality of a representative page. It is commonly assumed that the heterogeneous nature of the personalities and movements assembled in the book invalidates, or at least seriously detracts from, its value as responsible criticism.[10] Our own analysis has based itself on a denial of this assumption. If the world contains enthusiastic partisans of the stream-of-consciousness, behaviorists, Protestant modernist theologians, and psychological "testing-teams" named Yerkes and Yoakum, as well as Whitehead and Joyce, then surely some categories of understanding need to be applied. Admittedly, if "application" meant only that the category "time-philosopher" was pasted on some name, or if, somewhat lazily, the condemnation seemed only a matter of guilt-by-association, then we could well dismiss the whole operation. But the vigorous particularity distributed throughout the book is its best guarantee not only of continuing life and usefulness, but also a vindication of Lewis' version of the artist as the truly revolutionary man of vision, as the preserver of differentiation and individuality.

In a moment of candor he acknowledges the interested nature of his campaign on behalf of a substantial self: "I, of course, admit that the principle I advocate is not for everybody. Many must seek and find in a mercurial surface change their principle of life and endurance: action and not contemplation is most people's affair; 'Personality' is merely a burden and hardship to many" (363). The recognition is of that responsibility which Julien Benda, at about the same time, was chastising the absence of in false *clercs:* their betrayal of the contemplative study of affairs which was their true responsibility.

Lewis' performance in *Time and Western Man* provides a new sense of what the advocacy of principles can mean in its relation to other intellectuals and to the rest of society; he was right to claim that "in that abandoned fortress, there is still much loot." The finest tribute to the book, perhaps to Lewis' work in general, came from W. B. Yeats in a letter to Sturge Moore. Yeats was recovering from a recent operation in a somewhat unorthodox and very Yeatsian way:

I defy the doctor, as I do in writing this letter, by reading daily *Time and Western Man* and *The Art of Being Ruled* and feel that henceforth I need not say splenetic things for all is said. He mixes metaphors in the most preposterous ways but he can write; he has intellectual passions, and of that there has been very little these thirty years. His last book is among other things Plotinus or some Buddhist answering the astrologers (the only believers ever persecuted by Buddhists). I do not always hate what he hates and yet I am always glad that he hates. There are always men like that. Schopenhauer can do no wrong in my eyes: I no more quarrel with his errors than I do with a mountain cataract. Error is but the abyss into which he precipitates his truth.[11]

CHAPTER 4

Utopia Gone Wrong:
The Childermass *and* The Apes of God

ALTHOUGH it is proper to classify or praise *Time and West-ern Man*, and in narrower ways both *Paleface* and *The Dia-bolical Principle*, as examples of destructive criticism, the de-structive impulse in each works in the service of certain values whose existence is threatened by powerful forces: the cult of time-philosophy, sentimental primitivism, or a romantic diabolism which amuses itself at the spectacle of Western cultural dissolu-tion. The values Lewis aligns himself with can be named in various ways: the Artist; vision; space; Classicism; the surface of things; a substantial self; an external world that is, unlike the mind, dead.

More important than any of these explicitly named values is the presence in the polemics of a strong ironist. Thoroughly and mag-nificently endowed with Tarr's "curse of humor," he uses it, how-ever, in ways unavailable to that character whose rattling of chains suggested he was scarcely emancipated from the bourgeois habits to which he eventually gave half of himself. The ironist of the polemics sets out to damage and embarrass the fortunes of certain fashionable doctrines and tendencies; his "system" re-ferred to in *Time and Western Man* is systematic only in that one attitude overlaps with and implies another. Abstracted from Lewis' particular application of them, the ideas seem such simple fare that one hesitates to speak solemnly about his philosophy. But within the contexts of specific arguments, assaults and satirical portraits, the values look attractively sane—especially to readers who are willing to admit a strong temperamental bias in their philosophic views, if the appearance, the surface of things, can be saved.

While these books and essays were appearing, Lewis was also writing what, with some hesitation, we term fiction—*The Childer-mass* (1928) and *The Apes of God* (1930)—that bears the closest relationship to the critical works contemporaneous with it. As mentioned earlier, the satirical impulse behind *Tarr* and the stories which make up *The Wild Body* is "metaphysical" (recognizing that it leaves much of *Tarr* unaccounted for); and the creations of this impulse are purely themselves. They resist any analysis in terms of what they represent or what type they embody; Hobson is Hobson down to the superfluous inches of his trousers; Bestre, Brocatnaz, and the other inhabitants of the Breton coast are elemental figures answerable only to their own wild bodies. As a correlate of this rugged individualism, Lewis' attitude toward them is breezily tolerant, often admiring. Even the "villain" Otto Kreisler is an object of admiration, of wonder, rather than the butt of humor. Dr. Johnson's fertile remark about Congreve's comedies having "in some degree, the operation of tragedies; they surprise rather than divert, and raise admiration oftener than merriment" is relevant to Lewis' creative effects in his early fiction.

With *Childermass* and *Apes,* the air thickens, along with the books, and becomes a good deal harder to breathe freely in. If, as T. S. Eliot has said of his own works, prose may deal with ideals while poetry must deal with actuality, then Lewis' "poetry" of the late 1920's is, unlikely as it may at first seem, located in these two novels. Although *Childermass* takes place outside something called the Magnetic City and has been termed a philosophical fantasy, its world is still the "moronic inferno of insipidity and decay" (*RA*, 169) that *Apes* renders and that contradicts whatever Utopian ideas seek to transform it. To distinguish between the critical books and the "creative" ones of these years is, of course, particularly difficult; and Eliot's distinction between prose ideals and poetic actuality must not be taken too rigidly—ideals and actuality are admirably fused in works of his own like *Four Quartets* or *The Three Voices of Poetry.* In Lewis' case it is only necessary to mention the gallery of rogues and monsters through which the critical books conduct us to be reminded of how certain effects are absolutely dependent on the writer's power of satirical creation. It is perhaps somewhat harder to see how the novels, preoccupied as they are with the world as a moronic inferno, can express those rational standards and values by which the inferno is satirized and ultimately judged.

Lewis was not, of course, the first writer to have difficulty in expressing positive values within a particular form; even in Swift's *Modest Proposal,* that exemplar of concealment and subtlety, there is a moment toward the end where, in what seems a sudden tiring with the game, the projector loudly announces "Therefore let no man talk to me of other expedients," and proceeds with a list of sensible ways to relieve famine without stewing young children. The ways are indeed sensible, but their literary expression becomes suddenly of little interest since the relationship between Swift and the projector is vastly simplified in the interest of making truth heard. Yet it is also true that by this time we have seen the projector do his stuff sufficiently well and are little bothered by this lapse in the way affairs are concluded.

Lewis' massive operations present other problems for the satirist who has shown himself in the critical books such a partisan spirit of certain values, for it is hard to see just how those books relate to the writer who in 1930 and beyond was arguing that he practiced "satire-for-its-own-sake," detached from any demands of the ethical will. That is to say, the relative airiness and high-spirited tolerance of the earlier fiction is now harder to afford. It is difficult to imagine Lewis putting in an afternoon routing Whitehead or Spengler, and then sitting down after supper purely and simply to amuse himself by indulging in some "fiction." [1] There are only a very few figures in either *Childermass* or *Apes* who are created simply for themselves as objects of wonder; rather than admiration our response to them is more often one of a cynical nodding at "*that* type" or, more basically, a comprehending of the springs and actions of this or that puppet.

The mechanical metaphor is in play as usual; the difference is that a character in *Apes* is not to be laughed at (as in *The Wild Body*) primarily because he is a human being and all human beings are in a sense laughable, but because he is an example of a particular kind of human perversion. The young "genius" of that novel, Daniel Boleyn, is directed to observe certain apes because of their invaluably representative value as specimens. The greatest satire then may be non-moral, as the apologist argues; but, insofar as a satirist becomes more intense in the scorn and disgust with which he views his victims and more alienated from the realization in society of his own utopian values, his satire becomes moral in a way it would have been needless and unthinkable for *Tarr* or *The Wild Body* to be.

This moral impulse is precisely what animates *Childermass* and *Apes,* and it should not be too hastily saluted as a step forward in Lewis' fictional art; as he was the first to argue, there are ways and ways of being moral, most of which he was convinced were unworthy of the true artist. Yet these immense and barely readable "problem" books had to be written; for, if Lewis had not climbed out so far on such a long limb, the more available triumphs of his later fiction would probably have been impossible.

I Childermass

Lewis devotes only a paragraph in retrospect to this "novel—if you can call it that," terming its history "the most peaceful of any of my books" because it dealt with heavenly rather than earthly politics (*RA,* 199). Since no prominent figure was tempted to identify himself with any character, the circumstances of its publication, unlike those of *The Apes of God,* were harmless and inoffensive. In 1909, however, Lewis was less philosophically genial about the book's reception when in *The Enemy* #3 he launched an attack on the practice of classifying widely dissimilar books as "fiction" and then of handing them over to the incompetent hands of "fiction" reviewers. The uncomprehending reception of a book like *Childermass* is regarded as the outcome of this practice.

At the same time Lewis, contradicting his later remarks in *Rude Assignment,* insists that, because of the revolutionary character of his fiction, it causes more offense than does "non-fiction" like *Time and Western Man.* The point to be made is in opposition to Lewis' estimation: *Childermass* does not look like a revolutionary book today, nor was it truly so in 1928 except in demonstrably superficial ways. In 1955, when Lewis finally published under the title of *The Human Age,* Parts Two and Three of the projected four-part work, its impulse and expression had altered so radically from what could be perceived in *Childermass* alone that the relationship between the two creations, separated by almost thirty years, is an extraordinarily thin one. Adverse criticism of the earlier book only establishes by contrast the power and importance of its eventual successor.

Childermass has no narrative interest to speak of. Its scene is "outside Heaven," although it is in fact much farther outside than anticipated: the opening paragraphs place the actors and also introduce the tone in which the most impressive part of the book is conceived:

The city lies in a plane, ornamented with mountains. These appear as a fringe of crystals to the heavenly north. One minute bronze cone has a black plume of smoke. Beyond the oasis-plane is the desert. The sand-devils perform up to its northern and southern borders. The alluvial bench has recently gained, in the celestial region, upon the wall of the dunes. The "pulse of Asia" never ceases beating. But the outer Aeolian element has been worsted locally by the element of the oasis.

The approach to the so-called Yang Gate is over a ridge of nummulitic limestone. From its red crest the city and its walls are seen as though in an isometric plan. Two miles across, a tract of mist and dust separates this ridge from the river. It is here that in a shimmering obscurity the emigrant mass is collected within sight of the walls of the magnetic city. To the accompaniment of innumerable lowing horns along the banks of the river, a chorus of mournful messages, the day breaks. At the dully sparkling margin, their feet in the hot waves, stand the watermen, signalling from shore to shore. An exhausted movement disturbs the night-camp stretching on either side of the highway—which when it reaches the abrupt sides of the ridge turns at right angles northward. Mules and oxen are being driven out on to the road: like the tiny scratches of a needle upon this drum, having the horizon as its perimeter, cries are carried to the neighbourhood of the river.[2]

Lewis' prose has never functioned more directly. An unobstrusively simple syntax authenticates the strange objects of this landscape, while the chilly remoteness with which facts are set down seems to free their establishment from any whims on a narrator's part. It might be a disinterested voice from heaven itself that speaks.

When Yeats wrote to Lewis in praise of *Childermass*, and referred to moments in the first part of the book that "no writer of romance has surpassed," he probably had in mind a passage such as the opening; nor is it surprising to find H. G. Wells expressing his "glowing appreciation" of the book.[3] As a writer of romance, Lewis' plastic genius comes into play as it stakes out the terrain on which action occurs: the ascent to the Yang Gate and the Bailiff's court (157–60), the various glimpses of Old England observed by Pullman and Satters during their "time-travel," and the occurrence of disconcerting spatial changes—all are managed with toneless mastery of recitation. The reader does not so much see objects laid before him in full concreteness, as he is invited to imagine their coalescence into moments of elegantly hard surfaces, slabs of material arranged with space-time aplomb. The technique has nothing to do with realism; everything is invented, nothing simply noted or observed. In this respect, Lewis' remark that the politics of heaven have nothing to do with those of earth could be accepted if we substituted architecture, or some other plastic term, for politics.

But, in fact, as Hugh Kenner points out, the politics of heaven as they reveal themselves in *Childermass* bear a striking resemblance to the politics of earth described in *The Art of Being Ruled*, while the philosophic issues raised point directly to the concerns of *Time and Western Man*.[4] There are also bows made in the direction of the *Enemy* essays, "Paleface" and "The Diabolical Principle." In addition, the styles of certain earthly writers, primarily Joyce and Gertrude Stein, are imitated. Lewis does not seem overly concerned with just how these several impulses toward romance, philosophical criticism and debate, or literary parody might cohere in a work of art.

As mentioned earlier, narrative interest is minimal: James Pullman is introduced against the landscape presented at the opening of the book and soon meets the preposterous Satterthwaite ("Satters"), who once was his "fag" at school. The first part of the book consists of their progress to the Bailiff's court and of Pullman's attempts to enlighten the rather stupid youth regarding the nature of the world in which they find themselves. Eventually they reach the theater where the Bailiff holds court to determine which of the gathered souls are fit to enter what most think is heaven—in fact, an equivalent of purgatory. At this point, Pullman and Satters largely disappear from the picture; and the Bailiff takes over, engaging in long arguments with his main detractors, Hyperides (most of whose arguments Lewis is obviously sympathetic with) and Macrob, a surly man of action. Abruptly the book closes, inconclusively to be sure; the Bailiff prepares to return to what he calls his "citadel of Unreality"; and Pullman and Satters determine to follow him in the hope of sneaking into heaven. On this not very firm or interesting sequence of events is grafted the intellectual substance of the book.

The results are not satisfactory. At one moment we have Pull-

man lecturing Satters on metaphysics in the style of Marshall Mc-
Luhan: " 'We are organic with the things around us. This piece of
cloth'—he takes up a pinch of his coat sleeve—'is as much me as
this flesh. It's a superstition to think the me ends here.' He taps the
skin of his hand" (146–47). The reader who has done his home-
work in *Time and Western Man* understands that Whitehead is in
fashion and that organic mechanism makes up part of the "moronic" unreality depicted. Later on in the book the Bailiff lectures
Macrob as follows: "Once more however—there is no *you* apart
from what you perceive: your senses and you with them *are* all
that you habitually see and touch" (280). With reason we feel the
"Once more however" is all too appropriate; the point has been
made and is now being drummed in.

Or *The Art of Being Ruled* comes into play as the narrator
(Pullman having been completely forgotten at this point) analyzes the Bailiff's followers: "Their class-life dominates them so
that their responses to alien stimulus would be impersonal class-
responses, or such as are proper to their prescribed function"
(309). The analysis continues in a way that differs from the earlier book only in its being poorly stated. In fact, a general vulgari-
zation of Lewis' ideas occurs in this book as he attempts to convey
them through the tricky forms of debate or incidental novelistic
conversation between characters instead of through the natural
medium of expository prose directed at an audience and delivered
by the writer himself.

To argue that the Bailiff and others mouth parodies of intellectual positions alien to Lewis hardly improves matters—why parodies anyway? It is also fair to ask how much acquaintance with
the critical books preceding it *Childermass* demands before it can
be read with comprehension. There is no satisfactory answer: on
one hand, much of the debate is likely to remain obscure to a
reader unfamiliar with *The Art of Being Ruled* and *Time and
Western Man;* the portrait of the Bailiff as a master time-
philosopher does not sufficiently emerge from the novel taken by
itself. On the other hand, as already suggested, a familiarity with
the writer's intellectual concerns and nemeses does not make their
dramatization—indeed, they are seldom even dramatized—any
more revealing. It is safe to say that there is nothing to learn from
Childermass that has not already been demonstrated much more

effectively and strikingly in the critical books. Apart from its interest as a piece of romance, or even more crudely, as astounding
science fiction, the book stands or falls on the success of its literary
parody and on its grotesque transformations of common experience into memorable shapes and meanings—transformations that
are more elaborate than the purely physical distortions Lewis de-
picts so well.

The styles parodied, or rather imitated since they are themselves parodies of true English, are—as has been noted—those of
Gertrude Stein and of the Joyce of *Work in Progress*. Lewis' relationship to these writers was very much on his mind in 1928; indeed, a large part of *Time and Western Man* had been devoted to
analyzing Joyce's mind and Miss Stein's tongue. Both writers'
styles were easy targets, and Lewis' credentials as a "stein-
stutterer" are in good order: "Pulley has been most terribly helpful
and kind, terribly kind and most awfully helpful. He has been
kind and in a sense helpful, though not so helpful" (55). And he is
clear enough about Joyce's verbal punning and allusiveness to
produce a respectable swatch of Finneganese.

More important with respect to Joyce's presence in *Childermass*
are the uses of the "Circe" section of *Ulysses* and its technique of
hallucination. The difficulty with Lewis' handling of such effects is
that, unlike their employment in *Ulysses*, they arise from no consciousness whose workings have been revealed in the book; indeed, Lewis' commitment to the external approach precludes such
revelation. So the "hallucinations" do not significantly take on the
colorings and images of a particular mind but are instead laid on
from outside—all too frequently with a palpable design upon us.
For example, during an interlude at the Bailiff's court:

The orchestra, assembled upon a trestle platform at the left-hand
corner of the enclosure, with a mixed Jewish and negro personnel,
begins tuning up on its 'cellos, xylophones, saxophones, kettle-drums,
electric pianos, hooters and violins. The negro conductor rises with an
imperious immobility, displaying his baton and flashing his eye upon
his instrumentalists. The overture to *Don Giovanni* is begun. The
minor chord of the opening is interpreted with traditional correctness.
After that, first with the connivance, then at the suggestion, and finally
in the midst of the furious insistence of the black *chef d'orchestra*, the
Mozartian allegro becomes effaced beneath the melting ice-cream

glaciers of the "Blue Rockies," lapped up by the chocolate-cream
breakers of the "Blue Danube," rounded up by a Charleston, rescued
momentarily by a jigging violin, lost again in a percussion attack.

(297)

Even if this passage did not involve some gratuitous minority baiting, it would fail as a piece of literary invention; neither the personnel, nor the instruments, nor the course of the piece incites
undue hilarity. But the reader acquainted with the *Enemy* essay
"Paleface" is invited to interpret the event by plugging it into a
category like "primitivism" or by putting labels together like
"Negro," "Jazz," "chaotic restless flux," and the design then comes
clear enough: in this time-world Negroes (and Jews, for good
measure) efface Mozart with the Charleston. Is this not what our
vulgar modern culture takes as reality? The "idea," unconvincing
as it sounds, is made even more sentimental by the superficial
ways it takes the name for the thing: everyone is in favor of *Don
Giovanni* (though, if Lewis had ever listened to it, he might not
have chosen for his "classic" image such a stormy work of flux);
and the Charleston is of course modern and therefore necessarily
a debased form of something or other. And with what predictable
frequency in Lewis' books the adjective "chocolate-cream" occurs
as a modifier for something disapproved of.

Compared to this rather fastidious and even finicky "classicism,"
Joyce's inventions in the "Circe" episode are truly comic—Bloom
eating a peck of oysters, supervising a race among elderly crip-
ples, or performing various miracles. There is a play in such free
invention that Lewis, concerned with embodying certain ideas in
fantastic transformations, is seldom able to achieve. Instead, the
presence of a heavy hand is often to be detected. What most distinguishes Parts Two and Three of *The Human Age* thirty years
later is exactly that free inventiveness which Part One—*Childermass*—lacks. The writer of romance, still brilliantly present in
subsequent volumes, is no longer encumbered by the parodist of
other styles or by the illustrator of his own previously expressed
notions—with the result that the novel develops its own creative
life. An enormous step had to be taken, the understanding of
which involves a close look at Lewis' fiction of the next decade.
But we must first consider the book he saw as culminating his
work in the decade about to close.

II The Apes of God

Lewis tells us that *The Apes of God*, like *The Art of Being Ruled*, is an account of "the decadence occupying the trough between the two world-wars" (*RA*, 169). It tours the "moronic inferno of insipidity and decay" but presents it without the element of romance that in *Childermass* takes away at least part of the curse. Next to *Tarr*, *The Apes of God* is probably Lewis' best known work, especially if, as in surveys of modern fiction, he is taken primarily—along with Aldous Huxley and Evelyn Waugh—as a postwar English satirist. Also the longest of Lewis' novels, *Apes* probably shares with *Childermass* the gloomy distinction of having been left unfinished by more people than any other piece of modern fiction. But its publication was a major literary and cultural event. The tributes Lewis managed to bring together in his pamphlet *Satire and Fiction*, which followed close on the heels of *Apes*, remind us that some intelligent writers admired the book; Eliot's word for the section of *Apes* that he published in *The Criterion* was "a masterpiece," and there were others as enthusiastic about the completed book.

The story of the famous "Rejected Review"—written by Roy Campbell and turned down by the *New Statesman* on the grounds that it was too favorable to the novel—can be gleaned from reading Lewis' letters and hunting up a rare copy of his pamphlet on satire, the theoretical part of which was later incorporated in *Men Without Art* (1934). In that work Lewis makes the grandiose claim that "The Greatest Satire is Non-Moral," the claim being a reasonable, theoretical extension of his own practice in *The Wild Body*. Otherwise the position taken with regard to satire is equally familiar: as the "truth" of the intellect, it is opposed to Romance; it will be humanly disagreeable to those who look at the world with private, rose-colored glasses; most important, it will, in Lewis' hands, concern itself with the externals of things rather than with what is contemptuously referred to as "the 'dark' gushings of the tides of *The Great Within*" (123). Efforts are also made to identify the truth and method of satire with those of natural science, and great stress is put on the objectivity with which satire regards man *sub specie aeternitatis* rather than as a creature of peculiarly individual and sympathetic local habits.

It is interesting, then, that in *The Apes of God* Mr. Horace Za-

78   WYNDHAM LEWIS

greus, chief ape tormentor and director of the revels, speaks in quite a different manner during perhaps the most authoritative "broadcasts" of his master's voice. The master, Pierpoint, does not appear in the novel; but his opinions are delivered by disciples among whom Horace is preeminent. In the midst of Lord Osmund Finnian-Shaw's "lenten" party, Horace provides the "split-man" Julius Ratner with a disquisition on the nature of satire: "True satire must be vicious, Hazlitt I believe was right, not wrong as is generally thought in accusing Shakespeare of being too good-natured" (450). Horace then maintains that venom, rather than laughter, is necessary; that the satirist must remain on the surface where things and people differ, rather than look within where they are all alike, and thus universally forgivable.

At the same time, this external approach must, if it is to be good satire, be "unfair and single-minded": "To the satirist a thing must present itself as more simple, it must possess a stupid finality, it must be more rigidly contained by its genera, than in fact anything is" (451). There is no basis for qualifying Horace's remarks: that he is but a mouthpiece for his boss, says nothing against the validity of the ideas mouthed, especially since they are more accurate rationalizations of Lewis' satiric practice in this book than the remarks referred to earlier, which were written after the novel had been published. Single-minded externality of treatment combined with vicious outpourings of venom: the modern prose-satirist needs both because the hides of his victims have grown so thick. Little is said about seeing mankind with objectivity *sub specie aeternitatis;* instead, the emphasis is on the most effective way to hunt down victims.

In explanation of why *The Apes of God* is a monumentally dead book, and such a description seems reasonable, critics often say that Lewis wasted his heavy artillery on trivial targets; that the embodiments of folly and viciousness in the novel are simply not worth the energy devoted to them. This criticism may mean that the book is too long or that it is pedantic in its detailing of manners. Most other satiric fiction published around 1930 that deals with similar varieties of apery is short, brittle, and deadpan in its depiction of shams: Waugh's *Vile Bodies* (1930) or Anthony Powell's *Afternoon Men* (1931) are admirable partly because of their superb pace, and they are relatively without venom. Yet these novels, alive as they are today, can not be compared with

Lewis' anatomy of trivia which set out to compete with *Ulysses*. By eschewing Joyce's corrupt method of internal narration, Lewis hoped to produce the *compleat* external satire; but *Ulysses* is a great novel—*Apes* merely a curiosity investigated by few.

The defect in *Apes* is not that its occupants are "too trivial" (whatever that may mean) but that Lewis has not succeeded in creating this triviality so that it can be apprehended in interesting and various ways. No doubt Joyce's Mr. Deasy, Gertie McDowell, and The Citizen are trivial enough on some absolute scale of life-importance; but their triumphant life on the pages of *Ulysses* proves the irrelevance of that criterion in judging novelistic success. Nor will it do to praise one method of narration exclusively at the expense of the other; although Gertie is revealed in part through the "dark gushings" of internal monologue, Mr. Deasy and The Citizen are as externally presented as any character in *Apes;* and there is a fair amount of conventionally rendered internal thoughts and feelings in Lewis' book.

As was the case with *Childermass*, little need be said about the narrative of *Apes*, which consists of a number of loosely held together episodes culminating in a three-hundred-page evening at Lord Osmund's party. The heroes are Horace Zagreus, disciple of the offstage Pierpoint, and Horace's protegé Dan, who is undergoing a course of instruction in the ways of apery. Their relationship recalls Pullman-Satters and is one that recurs in Lewis' fiction: the authoritative and intelligent figure leads about his younger and more-or-less foolish student-child. Dan follows instructions, goes to tea parties with or without his tutor, and is eventually shelved by him when he has run out of that "genius" Horace had convinced him was his youthful possession. That Horace, unlike Pullman, is capable of immense foolishness in his speeches about Dan's "genius" ("You are a child of the Moon, when I first set eyes on you I knew it, you possess the *virtus vegetandi*" [117]) is putting it mildly; but, though various characters suggest that Horace is homosexual, there is little basis for seeing him as the object of satire since only through him can the society of apes be anatomized.

Behind Horace stands Pierpoint, revealed largely through an extract from "The Encyclical" he had once presented Horace. "The Encyclical" develops notions from *The Art of Being Ruled*, delineating the unpromising conditions under which true artists practice. The "societification" of art, the cult of the amateur, the child artist, and the replacement of talent by money as the qualification for membership in bohemia are accomplished facts. Pierpoint's (and Lewis') claim is that those who have accomplished this takeover are Apes of God; parasitically imitative of true art which they affect to admire but really despise, their activities are a hateful parody of it.

The sentiments expressed in this encyclical are well and good, but we wonder if they have very much to do with the manner in which individual apes are presented. For example, we have this typical piece of descriptive writing from the section titled "Lesbian-Ape" in which the lumbering Dan wanders by mistake into the apartment of a hard-boiled specimen of the new dispensation: "She was wiry and alert with hennaed hair bristling, enbrosse. In khaki-shorts, her hands were in their pockets, and her bare sunburnt legs were all muscle and no nonsense at all. . . . The bare brown feet were strapped into spartan sandals. A cigarette-holder half a foot long protruded from a firm-set jaw. It pointed at Dan, sparkling angrily as the breath was compressed within its bore" (222).

Compared to other more highly energized descriptions in *Apes*, this one is mild; but it leaves little doubt about the sort of customer Dan is up against. He is taken for a model, made to strip and pose until, overwhelmed with shame and a violent headache, he makes his exit. The not overly subtle episode is made interesting by details such as the half-foot cigarette lighter that sparkles angrily at Dan; there is absolutely no temptation to see the lady as an "illustration" of Pierpoint's theory, or as an object of satire that must be assaulted with viciousness and venom. We need a better word than "satire" to describe the verbal impulse that puts Lesbian-Ape before the eyes. Lewis, like the Dickens whose presence is felt so often in his works, is a greatly endowed entertainer, a showman whose stock of invention sometimes seems inexhaustible; the creation here is as genially free as anything in *The Wild Body*.

But, as suggested previously, the book was written out of disgust with the sham art world of the 1920's. Thus Lewis faced a problem: if the characters were created with free and independent identities, they would be invulnerable to any judgment passed upon them by author and reader, in which case the committed

satirist became just another brand, if a very good one, of entertainer. As if to guard against the presence of such uncontrollable
wild bodies, Lewis went to the other extreme by bringing in figures whom he (and Horace) could nag and abuse. One of these is
the aforementioned split-man himself, Julius Ratner, who is so
thoroughly unpleasant that even his physiological condition on
arising must be fully discussed: "And now the morning eye-glue
of yellow-lidded, sleek-necked Joo, was attacked by the tear-
glands which he had. This was but a desiccated trickle because
Joo was a parched wilderness of an organism so much more col-
loid than aquatic" (144).

In this elephantine manner, he is sneered at throughout the
novel in ways that rarely vary. The reader can only agree wearily
that Ratner is a sham, but it is hard to see any purpose behind the
elaborate pedantry of attention directed at him. The pedantry is
also felt in prolonged conversations about nothing that are held
by Lord Osmund and his friends, Ratner and his charwoman, or
the group at Pamela Farnham's tea party. By omitting commas
and collapsing the sentence, Lewis seeks to convey the rhythms of
inanity; yet his own tolerance for them is perhaps higher than the
reader's. Joyce, whatever reservations about some of the experi-
ments in the later parts of *Ulysses*, is at least trying something
new; Lewis repeats himself, both at the level of ideas and of technique. If it is said in reply that so does this world repeat itself,
there is little to do but invoke the fallacy of imitative form.

What *The Apes of God* most needs is to have something happen—anything to break the pattern of triviality and to gather the
tremendous energies of the book into some focus of significance.
When Stephen Dedalus swings his ash plant in the brothel at the
climax of "Circe," the event may be something less than "the ruin
of all space, shattered glass and toppling masonry, and time one
livid, final flame" of his earlier romantic imaginings; but it *is* an
event from which the rest of the novel can fall away. Since no one
in *Apes* is permitted a heroic aspiration and since in fact no one
even hears anybody else, the book can only go on and on. What
might have been a magnificent stroke—ending the book with a
picture of London on the morning of the General Strike—does not
succeed; for the scene is viewed through the (by this time) in-
sufferably tedious consciousness of Dan the moron, who is engaged only in avoiding men who offer him lifts. Somehow the

apes need to be gathered together for one last time—perhaps it would take Proust to do it—and faced with Horace and Pierpont.

But we cannot write the novel that is not there; these remarks, intent as they have been on suggesting why *Apes* is not satisfactory, have possibly been premature in applying judgments about Lewis' success or failure. The balance can partly be righted by a look at the book where it is strongest and where it raises the possibility of a dramatic confrontation between Horace and the apes that never quite occurs, although the curious relationship between them is explored. The confrontation does not occur in the long and frequently boring concluding section—the party at Lord Osmund's—but in an earlier section titled "Chez Lionel Kein, Esq.," which stands out from the rest of the book by its serious dependence on some promptings from "The Great Within," and by the cumulative way that it hints of the strangeness and terror lying just behind social relationships. It begins with an arresting image:

Mr. Zagreus stared at his imposing shadow moving slightly upon Kein's door. He steadied himself against this exenterated papier-maché self, dodging parallax as it moved with the precision of its contingent nature —registering the slightest breath of life disturbing the higher dimensional shape it waited upon. *On ne mesure pas les hommes à la toise!* Dan's shadow, as well, waited upon him, not upon its original. Dan was there like a shadow too, on and before the door. Were they inside the door as well, in further projections of still less substance—their stationary presences multiplied till they stretched out like a theater queue? Was there anything after the shadow (as was there anything behind the man)? The queue of four might be multiplied to any power within, from where still no sound issued.

(237)

The relatively grave and speculative manner in which the reflection occurs indicates something out of the ordinary. Perhaps since it is the Keins, fervent worshipers of Proust, who are being visited, the narrative is paying its respects to their hero; at any rate, Horace answers his own question. We can assume the presence of a consciousness "behind the man" analyzing the man's movements; for an interesting moment this novel about the externals of things reaches out in imagination to a ghost in the machine, a mind that might even be a source of independent interest. Lewis seems either unaware or uninterested in this possibility, though it lurks in his ambiguous use of the word "behind"; instead, Horace's rather more distressing reflection concerns the endless extension of mimic shadows in which he and Dan take their place.

The chapter begins, in other words, with a moment when the competent Horace suddenly lacks his usual firm grip on the external world. This note recurs throughout the episode: Horace engages in a long debate about Proust with the Keins, then proceeds to act at lunch like a Proustian intelligence who critically anatomizes the guests and the hostess herself until she bangs down her fist and tells him to leave. A number of things are going on in the extended debate. First of all, Lewis is attacking the confusion of art and life as it is embodied in the Keins, who would love to be characters in Proust's novel. Against this tendency, Horace ("broadcasting" Pierpoint) argues that any great artist-novelist would turn such a harsh spotlight on a "real person" that the person would find his fictional character unbearable—unless, like the Verdurins, he would be too stupid to see it. The realms of art and life are confused and dissolved into each other only by the false artist, a purveyor of high-class "Fiction" who is really a clever gossip and who writes novels to slander his enemies (the bad characters) and to idealize his friends (the heroes).

Though such fiction may clothe itself in the doctrine of impersonality, the novels that result will be very personal indeed. This, Horace suggests, is Proust's legacy, handed down to the likes of Lionel Kein, whose novels are written in company with his wife and whose titles include *Mayfair. Six double O.* At lunch the guests are seen by Horace as sixteen characters in search of an author (Pirandello has just been mentioned); each has been written about in the other's book and taken from "real life" in a depressingly literal way. So each is a character, laboring under his false-author but awaiting the great artist who will effect a truly imaginative transformation of feeble reality into immortal life: "What a sigh of utter relief there will be—when the Ape can cease from Aping, and the sham artist lay down his pen and brush and be at rest!" (294).

As a broadcast this one does not differ significantly from others engaged in by Horace-Pierpoint-Lewis, but its attendant circumstances are such that instead of coming across as simply a piece of propaganda, or a truth to be contemplated in detachment from the events of the novel, it is implicated with those events. For, as

Horace is pontificating to Dan, he hears the hostess, Isabel Kein,
traducing him to one of her guests as a "peculiar" person, in fact
as an albino; and he thereupon makes sarcastic mention in his
own speech of that "well-bred" and "cultivated" hostess. Horace's
pretensions to a vantage point outside the ape-world from which
he can criticize it are thus seriously called into question. There
follows an exclamatory meditation in which he calls himself to
account before proceeding to wage further war with Isabel. We
are brought back suddenly to the opening paragraphs of the section:

. . . *The theater-queue had come to life,* now: here, all about him,
in solid ranks, it chattered and ate. He had imagined a queue. But
here it must be—less resembling the original—shadows upon the walls
of Pompeii, of Paris, the hot andean plains—a horrible family of shadows. An ape-herd, all projections of himself, or he of them, or another
—gathered from everywhere, swarming in after him, or collected to
await him. Their plangent personalities, stuck up in opposite rows, be-
haved as though they were meeting for the first time (as indeed they
might be) and had little connection. . . . Or the queue had started
acting—for want of an author, as he had just said—after a fashion.
When their eyes met his it was always *himself,* in some form, at some
time.

                                                        (295-96)

It is rather difficult to say just where Lewis stands in relation to
his hero at this moment, but the tone of the meditation guarantees
a high degree of imaginative involvement in Horace's plight. In
fact, the analogy between character and creator is a very strong
one: as Horace's objective analysis of the apes is qualified by his
personal involvement with them—as he becomes for the moment
a Proustian narrator who is a part of all he surveys rather than
apart from it—so Lewis the "external" satirist seems to be imagining the great obstacle to such an art—an author's sympathetic
identification with his characters. This limitation, as we saw earlier, was Shakespeare's as a satirist: he saw too deeply, accepted
too many kinds of life, was not vicious enough. On the other hand,
the sympathy that threatens to overwhelm both Horace and his
creator has little to do with understanding and tolerance; it is
viewed rather as a horrified guilt-by-association that no detachment can overcome. We must be wary of providing a more ex-

plicit statement of the situation than is clearly on the page, yet it is difficult to account in any other way for the powerful impact of the passage, and of the whole section. In a way, it vindicates the book.

The Apes of God, like its satirical ancestor *Vanity Fair*, is a novel without a hero, in Thackeray's sense of the term. Horace Zagreus is usually treated in a manner that makes questions about his soul impossibly absurd. And Lewis is as evasive and uncertain as Thackeray was about the possibility of combining a satiric treatment of apery or vanity with a moral judgment and condemnation of it. Only Pierpoint, the man who is not there, can really know this world; the conditions for such knowledge seemingly are that the knower cannot be a character in the novel. With Zagreus, Lewis plays it now this way, now that (as does Thackeray with Becky), depending on the exigencies of a particular moment, or sometimes his own peculiar whims. His compulsive sneering and leering at the travesties of human nature that he creates is as much a loud diversion of attention from the novel's real significance as is Thackeray's patronizing care of Amelia or Dobbin.

When Horace is finally abandoned in the final pages of the book to the withered arms of Lady Fredigonde with whom the novel began, the gesture is as equivocal and meaningless as the puzzling treatment of Becky in the final chapters of *Vanity Fair*. Both careers are extreme simplifications of what had earlier been complexly dealt with. These more complex dealings are what Lewis attempted to give his heroes in the novels that followed *The Apes of God*, and it is perhaps in relation to those novels that the book may legitimately be seen. In this sense, it fascinates by the way it puts questions to the satirist that are not put by theoretical talk about "external" or "non-moral" satire such as is found in *Men Without Art*. In fact, the most revealing criticism of the monument to apery is contained within itself.

CHAPTER 5

Lewis as a Literary Critic

> In the arts of formal expression, a "dark night
> of the soul" is settling down. A kind of mental
> language is in process of invention, flouting and
> overriding the larynx and the tongue. Yet an
> art that is "subjective" and can look to no com-
> mon factors of knowledge or feeling, and lean
> on no tradition, is exposed to the necessity, first
> of all, of instructing itself far more profoundly
> as to the origins of its impulses and the nature
> and history of the formulas with which it
> works; or else it is committed to becoming a
> zealous parrot of systems and judgments that
> reach it from the unknown.
>
> *Paleface*

AS Lewis worked to complete *The Apes of God,* his own monstrous parody of twentieth-century "mental language," he
became increasingly committed to the instructing of his literary
contemporaries. Much of this instruction went on in the three issues of his one-man magazine, *The Enemy,* and made up a significant part of *Time and Western Man, Paleface,* and *The Diabolical
Principle.* Then, after publication of *The Apes* and the violent
abuse Lewis felt it brought on him, he wrote a number of extremely disenchanted articles and collected them in the gloomy
and brilliant *Men Without Art.* Within these eight years (1927–
34) we have a body of polemical writing which, when sifted and
combined, makes a literary criticism consistent and intelligent
enough to be admired—certainly recognized, as it is not at the
moment.

If the term "literary criticism" suggests a discipline more academic, or at least more settled and measured than Lewis pre-
tended to, it is justified if certain reservations are made. Lewis

wrote no essays in literary appreciation or explication for its own sake, and he had no interest in evaluating or ranking writers and their books. Nor, with the exception of *The Lion and the Fox*—a book in part about Shakespeare, though not really "on" Shakespeare—does Lewis' criticism address itself to writers of the past. There is a chapter on Henry James in *Men Without Art*, but he is invoked mainly for the light he can throw on the contemporary novel. To be alive and very much engaged in writing seems almost a requirement for consideration; the past is invoked only for what it tells us about where we are or are not in the present.

Moreover, Lewis' criticism deals almost entirely with the novel or other prose. He felt, one gathers, that poetry was an admirable enough affair, if a good deal less in touch with modern reality than the novel; the result is that the only modern poem he ever criticizes, and that only to point out certain mannerisms of Pound, is the *Cantos*. Although Lewis shows himself an astute close reader of a page of Hemingway or an Eliot essay, there is no interest in subjecting Eliot's poetry to such scrutiny. It may well have been that he was conservative (and self-protective) enough to feel that the critic of a medium should be an interested practitioner of the one he criticizes; and Lewis was hardly a poet, *One-Way Song* notwithstanding.

These limitations accepted, we may see Lewis' achievement for what it was. If, at first glance, its lack of critical disinterestedness raises doubts about its value, the doubts do not bulk so large when we look for such disinterestedness in the work of his best critical contemporaries. Admittedly there is an idea, a principle to advance or condemn, lying behind (usually not very far behind) every paragraph Lewis wrote about Joyce, Eliot, or Pound. But in anyone's list of the most valuable critics of modern literature—a short one might include Eliot, Lewis, Pound, and D. H. Lawrence—how often do we find the pure intelligence operating with Arnoldian objectivity to see the object as in itself it really is? What we find instead are strongly held convictions about what constitutes a healthy art and civilization, and a resultant concern with whether a specific book or writer promotes that art and civilization.

If added to this group, Lewis takes his place in the unlikely company of Pound and Lawrence, rather than with Eliot and Leavis whose critical achievements are immense and indisputable.

Compared to them, Pound and Lawrence sound like wild men, inclined on occasion to rant and to say foolish things, but also striking off brilliant and unsystematic perceptions about literature. It is probably with Lawrence's essays and reviews that Lewis' critical work can best be compared; both men practice criticism by fits and starts since something else important is forever intruding into their not-so-well-turned essays. Both are exceedingly—many would say excessively—personal critics, who excel in reading between the lines and bringing out the assumptions which underlie a given book. Once there, the assumptions often being anathema, they are subjected to high-powered irony that moves toward exposure of the falsity, vulgarity, banality of the book. And so perhaps it is fitting that each typed the other as a slave, respectively, of the intellect or the blood, and bracketed the other with an inferior, much more slavish partisan of those causes.[1]

Traditionally, Lewis, Pound, and Eliot are listed as men of the Right; however, Lewis' differences from the other two are fully as significant as the similarities, particularly as they bear on literature. But it has not been noted that Lewis' critical work has profound affinities with the literary-sociological interests of Leavis and the *Scrutiny* group in its early years. Although Leavis immortalizes him in the Richmond lecture as "the brutal and boring Wyndham Lewis," they were stalking many of the same enemies and tendencies in the years around 1930. With regard to the Sitwells, or Arnold Bennett's book reviewing, or the Joyce cult, they spoke as one voice—but, officially, they either ignored or dismissed each other.[2]

Although the usefulness of Lewis' criticism does not have to be defended on historical grounds, his ability to speak out fully and suggestively on *Ulysses* in 1927, or on Pound's "work in progress" in the same year, or on William Faulkner and Ernest Hemingway soon afterwards, shows that Lewis had an eye for the books that mattered and that would be influential. For that very reason it was important that they be subjected to a harder and more searching examination than any reviewer gave them. The following passage from the introduction to *Men Without Art* contains nothing to which at present we do not immediately assent. But said in the early 1930's, the statement reminds us that only through the efforts of practicing literary sociologists like Lewis, the *Scrutiny* group, George Orwell, and Edmund Wilson has it become the main assumption behind our criticism and teaching. The debt of the passage to I. A. Richards' *Principles of Literary Criticism* and to Eliot's work in general is evident:

All forms of art of a permanent order are intended not only to please and to excite . . . but to call into play the entire human capacity— for sensation, reflection, imagination, and will. We judge a work of art, ultimately, with reference to its capacity to effect this total mobiliza- tion of our faculties. The novel is no exception to this rule. . . .

Implicit in the serious work of art will be found politics, theology, philosophy—in brief all the great intellectual departments of the hu- man consciousness; even the Plain Reader is aware of that in theory. But what is not so clear to very many people is that the most harmless piece of literary entertainment . . . is at all events politically and morally influential.

(8–9)

But Lewis' main interest was not in exploring what he goes on to call the "whole barbarous system of conduct and judgment to match, [that] is *implied* in every flick of the kinetic novelettes"; and he turned instead to the more difficult task of bringing out those subtler implications found in the serious work of his con- temporaries.

I *The "Men of 1914"*

Even as it exposes certain tendencies in their work, Lewis' liter- ary criticism is at its most genial when it deals with those other members of what he termed the "Men of 1914"—Pound, Joyce, and Eliot. His remarks about this combination show as much warmth and loyalty, even pride, as he was likely to give to any group.[3] An unabashed pleasure in the highbrow aspect common to the art of all four writers—including Lewis—goes along with an explanation of why in 1937, when he published his reminiscent sketches of the "men" in *Blasting and Bombardiering*, that art had gone out of fashion. Lewis claims boldly that by contrast to Shaw, Wells, and even Oscar Wilde—all of whom were public identities to which the pursuit of art took second place—Joyce, Eliot, Pound, and himself "represent an attempt to get away from ro- mantic art into classical art, away from political propaganda back into the detachment of true literature" (252).

This attempt, he admits somewhat ruefully in 1937, did not quite succeed; but it failed only because the world with its wars, revolutions, and economic depressions had lost interest in art. The men of 1914 should therefore be regarded as *"the first men of a Future that has not materialized"* (258). Although the defiant nostalgia is well enough suited to the colloquial ease of an autobiographical memoir, it need not obscure the truth that the Men of 1914 marched with no such unity as Lewis later claimed they did. In fact, his particular claim that it was a "classic" as opposed to a "romantic" movement sounds out of place with Lewis' earlier practice, in analyzing the writings of these men, of exposing their romantic predilections—and therefore vices.

A   *Pound*

The simplest and most amiable instance of this tactic is the criticism of Ezra Pound found in separate chapters of *Time and Western Man,* one of them titled "A Man in Love With the Past." Various tributes to the kindness of Pound's nature as a living individual are interspersed with an assessment of his virtues and limitations as a poet. As a poet, Pound is "without a trace of originality of any sort," a "great intellectual parasite" (though not at all an unpleasant one) living off truly original artists; and, because of his allegiances to so many figures and times in the past, he is an "extremely untrustworthy guide to the present" (85). What Lewis in *Men Without Art* calls Pound's "tendency to regard a scuffle in fourteenth-century Siena as fundamentally more interesting than a similar scuffle in Wigan or Detroit today" (73) marks Pound's orthodoxy in the romantic cult of faraway places, and incidentally contradicts the memoir's suggestion that Pound is a "classic" artist. But there are also strong positive gifts that complement the limitations: Lewis notes Pound's uncanny ability to "get inside the skin of somebody else, of power and renown, a Propertius or an Arnaut Daniel" (86) and praises his superb capacities as a translator and imitator of other men's styles. In line with this comes the suggestion that the insincerity or falseness often heard when Pound speaks in his own person is a measure of that poet's inability to apprehend himself or other people as individuals: he is happier when the individual can be converted into a satirical type or an illustrative instance of some public category.

As a practical critic of the *Cantos* (nineteen of which had appeared when *Time and Western Man* was published), Lewis writes three pages which should be required reading for any student of Pound. He points to Pound's habit of expressing himself in a "mock-bitter sententious terseness" seen on one level in the "Amurrican" fondness for words like "bunk" and "slush," on the other, by a manneristic "breaking off" in the middle of a line. Anyone who breaks the pentameter today is likely to be regarded as at least on the right poetic track; Lewis, forty years ago, gave another name to certain effects in Pound's procedure with the verse-line, when he spoke of the "histrionic pausing" in parts of the *Cantos,* and labeled it as another aspect of Pound's romantic (if superficially classical) affiliations. The value of speaking in such a rough way about Pound's verse, particularly about what on a later occasion Lewis would refer to as the "admirable" *Cantos,* is that it frees one from being merely intimidated by all the rich, strange objects and people whom the poet knows. Lewis suggests, by implication, that the line between a passage from the *Cantos* which succeeds, and one that seems only pretentious name-dropping or chic time-travel, is a thin line that should be carefully inspected.

No such careful inspection is called for by what Lewis terms the "ole Ez" aspect of the poem: "So I sez wall haow is it you're over here, right off the champz Elyza?" Lewis simply calls this Pound at his worst, the poet as heavy-footed, boring, Teutonic clown. With a sort of comradely air of advice he suggests that, since Pound is so interested in music (his fervent championing of George Antheil is mentioned), he should get out of poetry and into a medium where he need have nothing to say. That would be preferable, Lewis claims, to using language in the manner of the Champz Elyza argot above; this and comparable passages "though they represent Pound the artist at his worst, they show us, I believe, the true Pound, or that part that has not become incorporated in his best highly traditional poetry. And a simpleton is what we are left with" (90).

Such a remark made in 1927 might look to be the merest arrogance, and to be mistaken to boot in view of Pound's dogged perseverance as the *Cantos* roll on. But just how mistaken is it? With the very important exception of the *Pisan Cantos,* where suddenly the poet creates an identity out of which he can speak, sometimes with great power, Lewis' judgment still makes sense. And it is interesting that the scene from contemporary life Pound was finally able to portray so affectingly involved putting the simpleton in a cage and exposing him to the world as a persecuted hero.

B *Joyce*

Lewis' criticism of Pound is a combination of admiration and condescension; in one paragraph he terms Pound a "kind of intellectual eunuch" but then shows how the limitation can also be a virtue: "He has not effected this intimate entrance into everything that is noble and enchanting for nothing. He has really walked with Sophocles beside the Aegean; he has *seen* the Florence of Cavalcanti. . . ." With Joyce, Lewis employs a somewhat related strategy, mixing respect and annoyance for Joyce's achievement into a highly creative criticism of *Ulysses.* "An Analysis of the Mind of James Joyce" makes up the major part of the "Revolutionary Simpleton" section of *Time and Western Man,* and *Ulysses* appears with Proust's novel as one of the two most important "time books" in modern literature. Yet the essay contains much observation about Joyce's mind and art that is independent of Lewis' war against the time philosophy; his perceptions about Joyce are simply more interesting than the idea in the name of which the perceptions are offered.

In brief, the analysis runs as follows: Joyce, like Pound, is a craftsman preoccupied with ways of saying or doing things, rather than an inventive, creative intelligence preoccupied with things to be done or said. He is technically progressive and humanly conservative; his passive receptivity to any stylistic wind is of a piece with his lack of preference for one particular point of view over another. His impartiality, then, is a defect in artistic personality, in individual identity. Again like Pound, although the point is not made explicitly, Joyce is an untrustworthy guide to the present because his present is the past—the accumulated Dublin rubbish of his young manhood. He has great sensitivity to verbal clichés, yet his characters are clichés of type rather than individuals; he finds it difficult to set before us a convincing identity that doesn't depend on conventional notions of race or class—the stage Irishman, the stage Jew. He looks, once more like Pound, through other people's eyes and not through his own. (How Joyce must have responded to the accusation of having second-class sight!)

In *Ulysses,* nineteenth-century naturalism combines with the passing parade of objects to form a great *nature morte;* the oppressive thing about it all is that the parade of objects is really one of reflections taking place in somebody's head and reproduced through internal narrative: in other words, Joyce has capitulated to the time philosophy. Lewis does not minimize the considerable achievement *Ulysses* represents; his metaphors boldly create the kind of achievement he takes it to be: "It is like a gigantic victorian quilt or antimacassar. Or it is the voluminous curtain that fell, belated (with the alarming momentum of a ton or two of personally organized rubbish), upon the victorian scene. So rich was its delivery, its pent-up outpouring so vehement, that it will remain, eternally cathartic, a monument like a record diarrhoea. No one who looks *at* it will ever want to look *behind* it. It is the sardonic catafalque of the victorian world" (109).

Aside from the impressively overwhelming nature of the description, its penultimate sentence is most important. *Ulysses,* Lewis is saying, is a book of the surface of things past, internalized into mental deadness, enveloped by thickly wadded words. In a sense, the book really doesn't *mean* anything ("No one who looks *at* it will ever want to look *behind* it"); and why should it, since its author has nothing to tell us, is not a mind at all, but a demon craftsman who is fascinated with doing things as many ways as possible. Of course, after Stuart Gilbert's book, most criticism of *Ulysses* has been very much interested in looking behind it, explaining and interpreting its symbols—even in supposing great wisdom was contained within if only the key to it all could be found; this criticism ignored what Lewis saw very clearly—the comic, encyclopedic nature of the book.

Only recently has Lewis' critique been recognized for the useful starting point it provides for discussion of *Ulysses;* that it is a beginning rather than a terminus is shown by the way critics who start from it arrive at very different estimates of the book. Hugh Kenner's *Dublin's Joyce* brought Lewis' critique into circulation by calling it, provocatively, a brilliant misreading. Kenner then defended the book as more thoroughly sardonic than Lewis realized; if Lewis thought Stephen Dedalus was a prig ("It would be difficult, I think, to find a more lifeless, irritating, principal figure than the deplorable hero of the *Portrait of the Artist* and of *Ulysses*"), Joyce knew it as well or better than anyone and liked him no better than Lewis did. If *Ulysses* was a vast glut of matter, a cathartic monument to the Victorian world, a record diarrhea,

Joyce meant it to be just that; he established Molly Bloom at the head of the flux and looked down in ironic mastery and mockery of it all. Kenner's argument is fascinating and unanswerable if one is willing to imagine a Joyce fully disengaged from his creations. But, as S. L. Goldberg demonstrates in *The Classical Temper*, Kenner's criticism simply turns Lewis upside down and transforms every apparent vice of *Ulysses* into a hidden virtue. By contrast, Goldberg's own reading of the book refuses to simplify Joyce's irony at its best into an either/or affair; instead, he looks behind the sardonic catafalque and finds, not mystic meanings, but a Joyce both sympathetic with and critical of his heroes, Bloom and Stephen. Like Lewis and Kenner, Goldberg sees the book as comic but finds the comedy a more humane one than do they.

This brief mention of one event in recent Joyce criticism takes us away from Lewis' own work, but demonstrates in a particular case how a critique lay around more or less unnoticed for twenty-five years, then became important to someone, and now appears as perhaps the most acute writing about Joyce done in the first few years after *Ulysses'* publication. That Lewis' account is tendentious, inconsistent with itself, perhaps inspired by motives of jealousy, general malice, or whatever one wishes to impute, may well be true; but it has stirred other readers to defense and rejoinder and is therefore alive today. Its most salutary assumption is that a novel exists to be read, responded to, and taken into our experience as a living book (even if it is a catafalque to dead matter), rather than treated as an exercise or puzzle to be figured out after we finish reading. The value of such criticism is inseparable from the partisan urgency of the beliefs and attitudes impelling it, and from the stylistic force with which the attitudes are expressed.

Unfortunately, few critics in 1927 seemed interested in taking up the challenge Lewis flung down: the result was that Joyce became either the high priest of a cult, or a newfangled "difficult" writer who might well hold unsound views. The long critique having concluded with some unfriendly remarks about *Work in Progress* ("He has fallen almost entirely into a literary horse-play on the one side, and Steinesque child-play on the other"), Lewis wrote no more on Joyce's art but confined his efforts to baiting the *Transition* disciples of the master.

C *T. S. Eliot*

The critique of Eliot, found wholly in the third chapter of *Men Without Art,* is still unnoticed; it reveals, I think, that Lewis was more fascinated and annoyed by Eliot's elusive person than by either Pound or Joyce, who, compared to the editor of *The Criterion,* were "mindless" craftsmen. Lewis felt that something very purposeful indeed was going on in Eliot's head at all times, and that the critic had thrown up a number of smoke screens behind which the (supposedly) anonymous poet could go on practicing his art. Lewis took it upon himself to expose Eliot; partly out of annoyance at what the writer was getting away with—what he was taken for by unwary readers; partly because Lewis was unsympathetic to certain artistic theories Eliot had successfully promulgated; and, although Lewis himself does not admit it, because Eliot was the most subtle pretender to "classical" status among the Men of 1914.

Lewis admits that Eliot's distinction and influence as a poet are profound, and he thinks it not a bad idea that his example has put the fear of careless writing into young poets. With this salute to Eliot's poetry out of the way, Lewis says nothing more about it; but, taking as his text some famous remarks from "Tradition and the Individual Talent" and the "Dante" essay, he sets out to examine the "depersonalization" or impersonal theory of poetry, and, bringing in I. A. Richards' work, the "disbelief" or pseudo-statement theory of poetry. These theories are related, Lewis argues: both Eliot and Richards have been preoccupied with the meaning of "sincerity" in poetry; both are deeply concerned with the problem of personality in art. Eliot in particular "has paid a good deal of curious attention to the sanctions required for the expression of the thinking subject in verse and prose" (68). This concern is understandable, since Eliot has purpose and personality about him; he is not simply exploiting one style after another with an indifference to what is being said.

The passages quoted from Eliot's "tradition" essay are two: one says that the artist must continually extinguish what is idiosyncratic to his personality and put himself in the service of a larger, more valuable consciousness of the past; the other draws a hard line between art and life by asserting that, when the poet does his job correctly, he is expressing a medium rather than a personality.

Lewis detects Pound's influence in the historical piety of the first
remark, but he finds the piety not quite so nobly impersonal or
"classical" as it appears on the surface. At this point, he makes the
already mentioned remark about Pound's preference of the scuffle
in Siena to the contemporary one in Detroit; so, even while Eliot
invokes the historical sense which recognizes not only the pastness
of the past but also its presence, Lewis makes the following important qualification: "But that past is, at the best, seeing its proportions, very selective, and its 'presence' is at the best ideal. You
cannot purge it of the glamour of strange lands. Strange times,
after all, *are* strange lands, neither more nor less" (73). The possible alliance of this historical attitude with the romantic temper
is what Lewis, still in his *Time and Western Man* mood, speaks
out against. He might well have gone on to mention *The Waste
Land* as a poetic indication of that temper, insofar as one cannot
agree with some commentators that the past is treated as skepti-
cally and disinterestedly as the present.

Lewis is equally distrustful of Eliot's insistence that the poet
expresses a medium rather than a personality. The "scientist" pretentions of the "Tradition" essay are brought out by a mischievous
suggestion that it has a good deal in common with Bertrand Russell's behaviorist account of the psyche—surely not an account
Eliot was anxious to support. More positively—and here the dis-
agreement expresses itself most simply and boldly—even in the
dark days of the 1930's there may still be *something* to say for that
much maligned entity the personality, at least as far as artist
rather than scientist is concerned: "I do not mean an individualist
abortion, bellowing that it wants at all costs to 'express' itself, and
feverishly answering the advertisement of the quack who promises to develop such things overnight. I mean only a constancy
and consistency in being, as concretely as possible, *one thing*—at
peace with itself, if not with the outer world, though that is likely
to follow after an interval of struggle . . ." (75). Such a defense
seems in part prophetic of the kind of coming to terms with self
that Eliot was to achieve in *Four Quartets,* a poem which in part
explores the continuity between the Man who suffers and the
Mind that creates.

Lewis' defense of the self is of a piece with his rejection of what
he terms the "disbelief" theory of reading poetry as developed by
I. A. Richards. As might be expected, the imaginative ability to

convert a poem's "truths" into mere "attitudes" and thus to enter into a poem no matter what it says, accepting or at least obediently entertaining its doctrine, was a notion of the ideal reader that held no interest for Lewis. It could certainly be argued that both Richards' "disbelief" theory and Eliot's impersonal one make their strongest appeal to youthful readers who are excited by the variety of literature and not very sure about what their own selves look like, or whether they even have a self. As the lines are drawn more firmly (Lewis was fifty-one when he wrote this critique), such imaginative tolerance may begin to look like diffusion or dilettantism. Both Eliot and Richards are expounding theories that do not promote the difficult attempt to be oneself, or to find out what that self may be. For this reason Lewis must argue that Eliot's insistence on impersonality is really a trick, that there are only ways and ways of being personal, and that one of them—a very subtle one—is to pretend one's poems have nothing to do with one's "real" personality. Eliot's position is a result, in Lewis' guess, of a theologically sensitive poet's effort to separate the admirable from the unsatisfactory in his personality, giving the former to art and perhaps—we may conjecture—asking to be forgiven for the latter in life.

In a revealing passage of summary Lewis both articulates his difference from Eliot and, incidentally, prefigures the increasingly free-swinging character of his own fiction:

The personality is not, I think, quite the pariah it becomes in the pages of Mr. Eliot: I do not believe in the anonymous, "impersonal," catalytic, for the very good reason that I am sure the personality is in that as much as in the other part of this double-headed oddity, however thoroughly disguised, and is more apt to be a corrupting influence in that arrangement than in the more usual one, where the artist is identified with his beliefs. If there is to be an "insincerity," I prefer it should occur in the opposite sense—namely that "the man, the personality" should exaggerate, a little artificially perhaps, his beliefs . . . the man is thus "most himself" (even if a little too much himself to be quite the perfect self, on occasion). . . .

The firm good temper and good sense of this passage are attractive for the way they let us know that Mr. Wyndham Lewis is not quite the perfect self, but very much himself, and that *there* finally is the temperamental basis for rejecting Eliot's theory.

Good temper, expressed through a colloquial ease that runs toward garrulity, unites with psychological acuteness about motives —the ability to imagine what other people are doing by reading between the lines they write or say.

Such intelligent good temper becomes especially apparent when Lewis' critique of Eliot is contrasted to a recent attack on the impersonal theory by F. R. Leavis, the critical insight of which is marred by its tone of bitterly moralistic reproof.[4] Lewis' essay, while it makes essentially the same point twenty-five years earlier, is notable throughout for its vigorous wit, most of which is inseparable from the strength of the point made. For example, he does not let pass without comment Eliot's denigration of Matthew Arnold in *The Use of Poetry and The Use of Criticism;* but, rather than content himself with high-toned reproof, or suggestions that Arnold was a finer critic than Eliot, Lewis simply notices that Eliot has coupled I. A. Richards with Arnold, both having had the temerity to hope that the world might be saved by poetry. The technique of guilt by association is rapidly exposed, not by heavy argument to prove that Arnold and Richards are treated unfairly, but through an instant deflation of Eliot's austere finger-wagging: "Mr. Eliot is *accusing* Mr. Richards of being like Arnold! Having degraded Arnold into the position of an inferior critic, to his complete satisfaction . . . it then occurs to him as an excellent idea to send people he does not approve of to join Arnold—like *sending to Coventry,* a little! Matthew Arnold becomes a sort of purgatory to which unsatisfactory people are dispatched . . ." (92–93).

Remarks like these provide the distinctive note of Lewis' critical essays. They are useful and liberating for the way they enable us to move from ostensible meaning to what is most likely going on behind the scenes. In this regard, Lewis' affection for the personalities of the "Men of 1914" and his rough sense that they were somehow allied, whether in instituting a classical revival or not, give his strongly adverse criticism a grace of tone that might even have recommended them to the writers under fire.

II *Novelists and the Novel*

Well, I do not wish to be offensive, but I do not see how situations such as these (Peace-situations, just as much as war-situations) can be treated in fiction, or in drama, or in any-

> thing else, without some degree of "coarseness"
> as it is called. Some are born "coarse," and
> some have "coarseness" thrust upon us. It is
> only by "coarseness" that we can paint our pic-
> ture truly.
>
> *Men Without Art*

This remark about coarseness has its eye on what Lewis calls "the disasters of the peace" to be observed in England and in the world in 1934—and perhaps in himself as well, as he moved into a prolonged illness and as his reputation, suffering from both *The Apes of God* and *Hitler,* began to sink. Lewis asks rhetorically if Goya would not have painted these disasters; in his own fiction he was preparing to paint them with a degree of unhighbrow-like coarseness largely absent from his previously "experimental" novels. The book that prepares the way for this fiction and that most fully documents Lewis' attitude toward the modern novel, is *Men Without Art;* grim-spirited, filled with magnificent comic touches, loosely constructed, rambling to the point of incoherence, it yields a fund of valuable perceptions about art in mass civilization.

If at times Lewis' own coarseness of approach to the Plain Reader is a bit too transparent—"I shall not mind, however, what is said about me if I have succeeded in leaving upon your retina a stain of blood, for the frou-frou vignettes of the next novel of the 'nice' school that you read" (253)—a generation brought up on the accents of Norman Mailer should find it familiar going. In fact Lewis' advertisements for himself are, like Mailer's, as objectively definitive of literary objects as they are subjectively fascinating. Rather than attempting to document what Lewis thought of this or that contemporary novelist, it is preferable to see how his remarks add up to a concerted rejection of idealism in the novel, and (again in line with Mailer's present impulse) "advertise" for an art that will be inclusive, therefore satirical.

A *Hemingway*

Men Without Art begins with a consideration of Ernest Hemingway, "a very considerable artist in prose-fiction," whose example both fascinates and appalls Lewis. He calls Hemingway's an art of the surface and of violent action; then follows an admiring analysis of his style as an art that conceals art. Lewis was the first critic of Hemingway to pay due attention to the stylistic trick which persuades us we are being given life, not art; yet, as with his approach to any artist, Lewis is interested in style only as it provides an unassailable indication of the ethics and politics of an era, as it permits him to move from the words on the page to the assumptions in which they are grounded. Put in terms of his preoccupation with time, the critical procedure can be seen as an effort to arrest the flux by reading contemplative, intellectual truths in it that it cannot know of itself.

Hemingway's work is conspicuous for its absence of politics (*To Have and Have Not* was as yet unpublished); and this absence, combined with the heroizing of the "dumb-ox," passive narrator to whom things are done, reveals something important about a world in which no novelist stands more highly than he. The assignment of such preeminence to Hemingway is partly a consequence of Lewis' defense of satire, which he strategically and exaggeratedly identifies with the whole of fiction. Modern fiction must be satirical since it must show us life in the third decade of the twentieth century; and, in the face of its own very probable extinction, it must "paint us a picture of what life looks like without art. That will be, of course, a satiric picture. Indeed it *is* one" (225). Hemingway has conveyed with great artfulness the world of men without art, and it is undeniable, I think, that his example is a strong influence on the proletarization of Lewis' own fictional style during the 1930's.

B *Henry James*

Lewis' program for the novelist-satirist of the 1930's involves the rejection of more complicated kinds of fictional "idealism" than the obvious varieties of sugaring met with in book-club happy endings. As we learn from inspecting the success of Joyce's *Ulysses*, the "internalist" psychologizing habit of mind has fully established its fictional credentials in the literary world. Henry James is addressed as the most distinguished example of a novelist who promoted the internalist cause by announcing that his main task was "the cure of souls" to whose interests the "picturesque" must be subjected—if necessary, even excluded. Lewis takes James' use of the picturesque to refer to objects, finds unnecessary and unhealthy his placing them in opposition to "souls" (Lewis' own habit being to convert "souls" into things), and classifies him as a writer whose novels have a paucity of direct action and gross substance. In a fine phrase he fixes James as an astonishing creator of "great disembodied romances" but wishes that he would mitigate this stifling, if rarefied, atmosphere by some externalist treatment of action and substance.

This inadequate criticism closes its eyes to the immensely satisfying amount of externalist rendering of things—the picturesque —to be found in *The Bostonians* and in other works of James' middle years; and the critic is in a weak position when he points to a habit as centrally defining as Jamesian idealism is, only to wish that somehow it were otherwise. But, as mentioned earlier, it is the tendency that James' work gave authority to, rather than the particular nature and merits of that work, which Lewis is concerned to isolate.

C *Virginia Woolf*

Lewis is on firmer ground and in full control of his argument when, in the chapter titled "Mr. Bennett and Mrs. Woolf," he deals with a true flower of idealism—a feminine talent for whose works he had little respect. The criticism of Virginia Woolf's imagination is made in the interest of coarseness, to which is opposed Mrs. Woolf's world of heroines who peep timidly and sensitively at the great masculine world outside them. Lewis ridicules and dismisses the rationale Virginia Woolf provided for herself in the famous essay "Mr. Bennett and Mrs. Brown." In response to her invocation of the Edwardians—Bennett, Wells, and John Galsworthy—as formidable and oppressive realistic novelists whom she (along with Joyce, Lawrence, Forster, and Lytton Strachey) were denying by their own complex, internal, and fragmentarily "poetic" art, Lewis scoffs at the coupling of robust imaginations like Joyce's and Lawrence's with the "paler" talents of Strachey and Mrs. Woolf herself. He asks also if there were not other novelists besides the three Edwardian "bullies" for a writer to turn to and receive confirmation from, and he wonders whether this version of literary history has perhaps been cooked up by Bloomsbury to justify the fact that the talents of its members are not of particularly impressive size or range: "as though she, Bennett, Wells and Galsworthy had been the only people in the world at the time, and as if there had been no books but their books, and no land but England" (66).

Clearly, Lewis is opposing this historical rationalization of

Virginia Woolf's in favor of his own interests as novelist; after all, when Lytton Strachey, rather than the author of *Tarr,* is coupled with Joyce as one of the movers in modern literature, then some mining operations on the landscape are in order and a brief appearance of The Enemy is a necessity. But the attack on Virginia Woolf and Bloomsbury cannot be explained away by calling Lewis' motives impure, since he succeeds in making a valid point about a certain kind of bad literary history.

He has no interest whatever in harking back nostalgically to the jolly old Edwardians, whose realism after all had few affinities with his own projected brand. Instead, the sentimentality and cultishness of "our" situation, as expounded by Virginia Woolf, needs to be exposed for the falsely profound but really evasive account which results: "If you ask: Do you mean then that there is nothing in this view at all, of ours being a period of *Sturm und Drang,* in which new methods are being tried out, and in which the artistic production is in consequence tentative? I reply: There is nothing new in the idea at all, if you mean that the present time differs from any other in being experimental and in seeking new forms: or if you seek to use that argument to account for mediocrity, or smallness of output, or any of the other individual 'failures' that occur . . ." (167).

This was strong talk for the over-susceptible Virginia Woolf (we learn from her diary that after reading Lewis' criticism she tended to be ill for several days).[5] But it is also admirable in its firm respect for the creative artist who must not be understood or pitied or excused by having historical categories applied to him— especially when he (or she) is scarcely yet a part of history. Lewis holds in contempt the air of wistful apology for one's inevitable limitations as a creative artist or human being; and, in a curious way, although he does not make the connection, such an apology is not so different from the Edwardian novelists' own version of things. Solemn deference to great impersonal forces that tower over the little lives of men can be as tediously invoked by Virginia Woolf as by Arnold Bennett or by C. P. Snow. By contrast, an art that is truly "coarse" has little interest in explaining human action by invoking forces, however palpable or unseen they may be. Lewis realized perhaps that Henry James' fiction never succumbed to these forces; and, though James may be of no use as an

influence on the kind of fiction Lewis would propagate, his example as an individual writer and as a free spirit was most salutary.

D   *D. H. Lawrence*

The kind of "idealism" represented by the writings of D. H.
Lawrence seems to have nothing to do with that of James' or Virginia Woolf's, insofar as Lawrence's object of veneration is "blood-
knowledge" rather than the cure of disembodied souls or ministra-
tion to the feminine consciousness. Lewis does not speak much of
Lawrence in *Men Without Art,* having devoted a large section to
him in the earlier *Paleface;* but there is no reason to doubt that his
adoption of what Lewis would call "romantic attitudes" toward
the primitive, the unconsciousness, and the blood, convicts him of
idealizing certain human propensities to the exclusion of others,
and therefore places him with the idealists as insufficiently
"coarse" writers—however full-blooded in one sense Lawrence
may be.

The treatment given Lawrence in *Paleface* is lopsided and over-
simplified since only one book, *Mornings in Mexico,* is discussed
at any length. From remarks made in passing and in other books,
we know that Lewis had little interest in or respect for what he
felt was Lawrence's doctrinaire message; however, Lewis' criticism becomes in places just as doctrinaire. For example, since
Sons and Lovers is about a youth, it reveals the motif of the "child-
cult"; or, in a description of Lawrence's attitudes, we hear of "a
hot and piping trinity of rough-stuff primitivism, and Freudian
hot-sex-stuff "(180). The hard-boiled quality of these remarks is
objectionable because of the way it puts Lewis on display in a
childish, mock-thuggish way; moreover, he refuses to ask whether
there exists anything besides "motifs" in Lawrence's novels, or
whether we are being asked by the critic simply to choose *his*
motif (the intellect) and belabor Lawrence's. Lewis writes, in
other words, as if Lawrence has no powers of analysis or criticism,
no capacities as a novelist; this attitude is absurd.

On the other hand, Lewis does point sharply and amusingly
enough to the vulnerability of the more rigid side of Lawrence as
it appears in *Mornings in Mexico* or elsewhere. Although Lewis
had Hemingway's *Torrents of Spring* to work with, he provides
some comic invention of his own by taking a Lawrentian sentence

in praise of the Redskin-feminine—"In woman virtue is the putting forth of all herself in a delicate, marvellous, sensitiveness, which draws forth the wonder to herself"—and imagining her husband's response: "What would the Indian think if he heard his squaw being written about in that strain?—'delicate marvellous sensitiveness.' He would probably say 'Chuck it, Archie!' in Hopi. At least he would be considerably surprised, and probably squint very hard, under his 'dark' brows, at Mr. Lawrence" (165–66). Not only was Lawrence capable on occasion of making this kind of criticism of his own doctrine (remember how, when Frieda began to exult in the horse's thighs moving beneath her, Lawrence told her she was talking rubbish and had been reading his books too much), but he himself was an expert at imagining what natural objects (or Indians) might say if they could respond to the sensitive poet's admiring of them.[6]

At this point the most sympathetic reader of Lewis' criticism may question whether it is not turning out to be the case that all novelists but Wyndham Lewis stand condemned as insufficiently "realistic" or "classical" or "satiric" or "coarse." There is some truth in the charge, yet Lewis was himself conscious of the monomaniacal possibilities of claiming to be the only really sanely disenchanted author in a deluded world of shams and illusionists. He recognized, and on one occasion in *Men Without Art* finely articulated it, that the world of the twentieth century made a mockery of any particular claim on the novelist's part to be a classicist, or "in the classical tradition," as opposed to his misguided fellow practitioners: "To be impersonal rather than personal; universal rather than provincial; rational rather than a mere creature of feeling—these . . . are very fine things indeed: but who possesses more than a tincture of them to-day? . . . With all of us—and to this there is no exception—there are merely *degrees* of the opposite tendency, at present labeled 'romantic'" (193–94).

Lewis' awareness here of his own "romantic" situation is of a superior order to his reiterated "classical" protests or harangues or boasts that he is on the side of the physical world, the surface of things or the "Great Without." Perhaps there *is* no common world left for men to share; and the artist's recognition of this fact makes understandable his withdrawal behind the veil into a world, it may be, of infinite fascination—or, looked at in a gloomier way, a "powerless, unsatisfactory, uncircumscribed private life" (*Paleface*, 102).

Surely Lewis' acceptance of an art that presents violent action, that shirks none of the material and spiritual disasters of the world, and that goes so far as to praise the saving coarseness necessary to convey these disasters, signals how remote from "classic" repose his own fiction will be. In his previous novels, no matter how violent and disturbed the presented actions might be, they were frozen into strange forms and shapes of meaning by the stylistic entertainer: as romancer, as "metaphysical" satirist, as parodist, or as other related identities. Whatever the result was, it looked like art, sternly highbrow and advance-guard. For the rest of his literary career the terms no longer apply, and we can recall a sentence of the quotation from *Paleface* which began this chapter: "Yet an art that is 'subjective' and can look to no common factors of knowledge or feeling, and lean on no tradition, is exposed to the necessity . . . of instructing itself far more profoundly as to the origins of its impulses and the nature and history of the formulas with which it works . . ." (103). The admonition is not simply one more rap on the knuckles of D. H. Lawrence or Joyce. Lewis' literary criticism was a bold effort to instruct other writers as to the origins of their subjective creations: the novels he was to write in the 1930's show him struggling to come to terms with the formulas and impulses of his own fiction. For the first time, he instructed himself as boldly as he did others.

CHAPTER 6

The Vulgar Streak:
Three Novels of the 1930's

BETWEEN 1931, a year marked by the infamous *Hitler* book, and 1941, when Lewis found himself uncomfortably settled in what he termed the "sanctimonious icebox" of Canada, some twenty books appeared under his name—or, rather, most of them appeared, if briefly. One was suppressed before publication and three after, due to the timidity of publishers in the face of either threatened or imagined libel suits. At present only one of the twenty titles is in print—*The Revenge for Love*—but, by any standards, the period contains more dross, more purely occasional and often careless work than any other in Lewis' career. Although our interest is in three novels that span the 1930's, a brief classification and an even briefer characterization of the remaining books is called for.

The first group consists of rewritten works, those whose material had been published earlier in essay form, and those best understood as documentation or completion of motifs sounded in the polemical books of the late 1920's. In this group are *The Diabolical Principle and the Dithyrambic Spectator* (1931), made up of two earlier essays; *The Doom of Youth* (1932), citing chapter and verse to demonstrate a thesis first developed in *The Art of Being Ruled* that the youth cult is a useful exploitation of social revolutionaries; *The Old Gang and the New Gang* (1933), supposedly written to fill the gap left by the suppressed *Doom of Youth*, but one of Lewis' poorest performances; plus much of the material on Romance and the exotic sense in *Hitler* (1931). A rewritten version of Lewis' play *The Enemy of the Stars* appeared in 1932 and is at least as unreadable as the first *Blast* version. Finally, *Wyndham Lewis the Artist: From "Blast" to Burlington House* collects some of his most valuable art criticism.

The avowedly political and contentious books, some of them labeled "anti-war" by Lewis in retrospect, form a second category to which belong the first Hitler book, *Left Wings Over Europe* (1936), and *Count Your Dead, They Are Alive!* (1937); then *The Hitler Cult* (1939) and *The Jews, Are They Human?* (1939). The last two works attempt to right the earlier praise of Hitler and to clear Lewis of charges of anti-semitism, but they are feeble and hasty pieces of writing, however sensible their attitudes may be. *Left Wings* and *Count Your Dead* could be supported or disputed page by page if we read the English dailies from 1935 to 1937 and found out what Stanley Baldwin actually said in Parliament on this or that occasion. It is enough here to suggest their limitations in contrast to Lewis' political novel of the same period. Hugh Kenner has an excellent discussion of the motives and deceptions behind Lewis' first book on Hitler,[1] and it should be added that what rankles in this connection is not so much that Lewis was taken in by Hitler's protestations in 1931, but that it took him eight years to change his mind. There is a general loss of focus in all of Lewis' writings about Hitler who is seen insistently as a sham but never as a threat, as a comic puppet but not as a scourge. But, since the whole matter has had much attention given it, there is little point in chastising Lewis any further.

Third, we have a relaxed miscellany consisting of the pleasant travel books *Filibusters in Barbary* (1932) and *America, I Presume* (1940); a repetitious disquisition on the English character, *The Mysterious Mr. Bull* (1938); and the volume of poems, *One-Way Song*, which some have admired. The unpublished, suppressed novel, *The Roaring Queen,* may be added to this list.

The fourth group contains the books for which Lewis should be remembered: the previously discussed *Men Without Art* (1934); the invaluable and affecting memoir, *Blasting and Bombardiering* (1937); and three novels: *Snooty Baronet* (1932), *The Revenge for Love* (1937), and *The Vulgar Streak* (1941). Lewis meant "the vulgar streak" to refer to his fictional hero's lower-class origins; we shall be using the phrase to characterize a new streak in that fiction. The difficult brilliance of *Apes of God* and *Childermass* becomes a thing of the past, like the 1920's; as Lewis' style coarsens and grows more "common," his moral feelings begin to clarify themselves.

The Revenge for Love and *The Vulgar Streak* mark a successful solution to the central problem of his literary career—that of the satirist's relation to life. They are the first books Lewis wrote since

Tarr (where the problem was initially raised) which have a beginning, middle, and end; they do not fly apart, but sustain their
relatively low-keyed narrations until a significant action has been
presented. When the book ends, it can be considered as an object
of contemplation instead of the projection or performance of a
clever author; indeed, "Wyndham Lewis" is more completely
identified with the novels themselves than he has ever been before
or was to be again. None of these claims holds good for the first
novel, *Snooty Baronet;* but a performance so curious and, at first
glance, so desperately trivial should be pressed for what it may
yield about the state of Lewis' fictional soul after it had suffered
The Apes of God.

I   Snooty Baronet

Readers of previous Lewis novels expect to do some hard work
in the first paragraphs, but there is nothing to prepare them for
the outlandish opening of *Snooty Baronet* in which an unlikely
figure, Sir Michael Kell-Imrie, is introduced in the unlikely environment of a New York City taxicab. A third-person narrative details with scrupulous intentness the appearance and movements of
an as yet unidentified personage—"The face was on-the-lookout
behind the window-glass of the taxicab. The left eye kept a sullen
watch: it was counting." Then, as this "black-suited six-footer"
emerges from the cab, the fake tension dissolves in a huge narrative *gaffe:* "The face was mine. I must apologize for arriving as it
were incognito upon the scene. No murder has been committed at
No. 1040 Livingston Avenue—I can't help it if this has opened as
if it were a gunman best-seller." Snooty "can't help it," because, as
he informs us, he is not only a baronet but a writer; and writers
are or should be embarrassed about beginning looks in the first
person. Besides, he has a wooden leg that renders him particularly
susceptible to a novel reader's criticism: "I could hardly say: 'The
taxi stopped. I crawled out. I have a wooden leg!' Tactically, that
would be hopelessly bad. You would simply say to yourself, 'This
must be a dull book. The hero has a wooden leg. Is the war not
over yet?' and throw the thing down in a very bad temper, cursing
your Lending Library" (2).

A good deal is going on within this super-casual prose that is
addressed, on one level, to the stupid devourer of novels who is
looking for a good "read." To him, Snooty speaks in full, slow-

motioned candor of the writer's difficulty in winning over a blasé public. Of course, *we* are not that public but readers of Wyndham Lewis, an author whose reputation in the lending libraries does not stand high; thus our relation to Snooty is rather more interesting. The pleasure and point of these opening paragraphs derive from their bluff inadequacy to any respectable literary situation; and, placed together in vapid sentences, the "ideas" of "dull book," "wooden leg," and "war not over yet?" combine in a parody of thought—the stream-of-consciousness at its most sluggish. That this bluff inadequacy also carries its peculiar charm suggests why the voice with which Lewis endows Snooty is not that of the hack writer to be satirized, but a voice by turns jaunty and ill-humored that lords it over the supporting cast of characters. Snooty, who admits he is a puppet, also knows that he is surrounded by puppets; and he proceeds to manipulate them with vigorous abandon.

The events following Snooty's introduction are every bit as preposterous. The first third of the novel—the only part we concern ourselves with in detail—catalogues the baronet's disgusted return to England; an evening spent with his mistress Val ("Old Valley"), culminating in sexual congress and its violent aftermath (Snooty becomes ill); and a talk with his literary agent "Humph" (Captain Humphrey Cooper Carter) in which Humph succeeds in selling the baronet on a trip to Persia, supposedly to investigate the origins of Mithras but actually to have Snooty captured in the desert by Arabs. From this romantic event a new, attractively heroic image of the writer will hopefully ensue. The section ends with a strange and vivid confrontation between Snooty and a hatter's dummy in the Strand.

The second part of the book is devoted to Rob McPhail, the poet-bullfighter modeled after Roy Campbell, who meets sudden death on a bull's horn before Snooty and Val can persuade him to accompany them to Persia. Finally, in Part Three, Persia is reached; and, after elaborate infighting among Snooty, Val, and Humph, the Arabs put in an appearance. As Humph waves good-by to the captured Snooty, assuring him he will soon be rescued, Snooty on an impulse raises his gun and plugs Humph twice. That matter taken care of, Old Val, with whom he is equally bored, conveniently contracts smallpox, at which point the baronet flies home to the arms of his lower-class mistress.

Hugh Kenner calls the novel a "joint-parody of D. H. and T. E.

Lawrence," [2] but T. E. (whom Lewis admired) has hardly been given equal satirical time with D. H., an old nemesis. At any rate, the unheroic desert incidents that conclude the book are too haphazard to bear much relation, even a satirical one, to *Seven Pillars of Wisdom*. D. H. is more palpably there since Snooty, taking Humph's tip about Mithras, finds a book of Lawrence's titled *Sol Invictus—Bull Unsexed* which he devours with undisguised excitement. This wholly imaginary book contains sentences like the following: "Mithras got all hot and clammy about the Bull . . . because he did not wish to kill the Bull at all, seeing that he loved it, passionately. 'Oh why must I kill Bullie-Woolie!' Thus spake Zarathustra" (92). The "parody" is so broad as to be harmless in the force of its satirical thrusts; and, just as the farfetched absurdities of the sentences make it certain that *Sol Invictus— Bull Unsexed* will be taken as a coarse joke of Lewis-Snooty's rather than as authentic Lawrence, so most of the wit in the book connects with nothing ouside itself.

Yet *Snooty* is a very funny book indeed, for it exploits a destructive wit that is close to childishness and that operates through the hero's silent ridicule of the language and gestures of those who surround and oppress him. The embattled heroes of Vladimir Nabokov's *Lolita* and Kingsley Amis' *Lucky Jim*, two recent novels admirable for their exploitation of this wit, show Humbert Humbert revenging himself on the philistines by abusing his wife ("Fat Haze") and twisting everyone's name to bits including his own; or, in the case of Jim Dixon, by making faces, imitating voices, and advising the hated Professor Welch's cat to "pee on the carpets." The natural alliance of childishness with silliness results in fictional qualities that disqualify the books for Leavis' great tradition; Nabokov and Amis are every bit as "hard-boiled" in their practice of this line of wit as was their precursor, Wyndham Lewis.

Snooty is most alive when the hero's imagination is busy compounding inanities in the face of his mistress' or his agent's behavior. When Val confides that a gentleman named "Mort" is paying the rent for her flat, and that she has indeed finally "got him in the bed," Snooty goes to work:

Fascinated (for the hundredth time, for if I had heard this once I had heard it far more than that) I saw the convulsive shadow of Mort—

I saw this wraith (I had never met him) struggling in THE BED—clutched with ten fluttering tentacles, of muscleless flesh, remorselessly closing in upon his impalpable substance—writhing in a delicious constriction. I heard the muffled panting of this fat shadow (for Mort was somewhat fat and short of breath) as he gave up the ghost. I felt the limp weight of his subsequent corpse, drained of its blood: and . . . I could almost perceive the dead weight, of the extinct Mort, sink down to the floor, like a stricken sausage-balloon, beneath the bullets of the Richthofen Circus—I heaved a long sigh at this harrowing spectacle.

"Well!" I said. "You've got him in the bed!"

(23–24)

As critic and polemicist Lewis always made the most of his fine ability to transform enemies into the heroes or victims of verbal fantasies, but he had never before allowed the hero of a novel such relaxed, confident word play. The atmospheres of *Tarr, Childermass,* and *Apes* are alike in that they will not admit of a slangy confidant to the reader. Although both Tarr and Horace Zagreus conceive themselves to be showmen, their performances are given in the name of sacred values; therefore, each takes himself with no little importance and is eternally reproving and correcting the misguided citizens of the world.

Snooty has his values too: he is a Behaviorist, an eager aspirant to the Mithraic revelation, an advocate of Nature as against Man, and of the cult of Action, and of Science in general. But, although Lewis holds these values in contempt, he does not, fortunately, attempt to use the novel as yet another full-fledged criticism of them. Snooty, like the heroes of Joyce's *Ulysses,* is filled with the most glaring deficiencies and absurdities, yet he has more life than the figures surrounding him, and he therefore wins our amused partisanship. At the end of the opening chapter, he reveals that his agent Humph, rather than himself, is in fact the hero of this book. When we met that "hero," he is done up in extravagant Dickensian fashion: "When I look at Humph's chin I am reminded of a strong-box. The chap is all chin. I hate this face more than I hate my own, which is saying a good deal" (57).

With that opening note, the chin proceeds to take over the chapter: it has a false bottom described in great detail; it can be used for the safe conveyance of dispatches and state documents; aspiring writers hope that this agent will fall head-over-chin for

their manuscripts; when Humph smokes his pipe, it looks as if the
chin is on fire; and at the moment when Humph is about to make
the solemn revelation of his Persian scheme, Snooty feels that
"The chin was now so much to the fore that we were both practically inside a chin rather than inside a room. *He had got me in his
Chin,* to parody old Val" (74). When the chin greets Snooty, it is
in the following manner:

> "*Hal*-lo!" he exclaimed hurriedly and shortly under his breath, meet-
> ing me at the door, staring at me in a great wooden unsmiling blank-
> ness, grasping my right hand just as it was escaping into a pocket.
> "I say, I hope you don't mind I've got *some.*"
> He'd *got some*—he'd got *some tea*—he'd got some sardines—he got
> *some* at all events—his wide-open eye fixed itself blankly upon my
> face, as he stopped at his *some.*
> "I hope you don't *mind* I've got *some*"—again he stopped, at what
> he had got—he allowed his voice to tail away at "some," to sink with
> discouragement until it was lost at our feet. Then cautiously he looked
> back over his shoulder, into the room, with puzzled hesitation. "I've
> got some people!"—All I've got is *pee*-ple, in mournful surprise he told
> me, dropping his voice still lower at *people.*
>
> (71–72)

Snooty's response to this bag of tics is usually a series of gaping
yawns (he yawns throughout the book); on this occasion, he
hums a bit of a song that runs "Nobody loves a poor fat girl, But
ah how a fat girl can love!" The music hall and vaudeville are just
around the corner, and the attention throughout is on Snooty's
irrepressible spirits as they are endowed with Lewisian inventiveness.

But, though the book is filled with a manic energy appropriate
to the Behaviorist inspecting tics, there is some doubt about
where Lewis stands in relation to the lively show he has set in
motion. Hugh Kenner's shrewd analysis of this relation maintains
that what began as satire ends as accepted truth: that the Behaviorist assumptions about human beings which were ridiculed in
Time and Western Man (the sections on Professor Watson and
the "testers") had, five years later, turned out to seem like such an
accurate description of human beings that "The only person the
behaviorist had insulted, it appears, was Wyndham Lewis." [3] In-

deed, there is even a moment when Lewis entertains doubts about his own privileged status—or at least as far as the analogy between him and his hero holds good. Snooty, in pursuit of an American club sandwich, suddenly finds himself face to face with a hatter's dummy in a store window. The chin is reminiscent of Humph, yet its extraordinary lifelikeness seems indistinguishable not only from the mechanical robots around Snooty, staring back at the dummy, but also from Snooty himself.

Kenner suggests that Lewis finally realized he had gotten into a fictional blind alley: "It is as though the narrator, having discovered outside the hatter's window the irrelevance of his mechanical contempt, lived out the second phase of his adventures and wrote them up to prove that even as a comic technique behaviorism could lead nowhere." [4] It is true that Snooty's adventures after confronting the hatter's automaton are meaningless and largely rendered without the inventive clowning of the first third of the book. Also, in the sense that "leads nowhere" indicates the novel's lack of any dramatic redefinition of motive and character, neither *Snooty* nor Lewis' previous novels have led anywhere: *Tarr's* questionings about the satirist's relation to life are begged by the close of the novel; Horace Zagreus has a momentary vision of the endless theater queue *chez* Lionel Klein's, but his speech and actions for the rest of *Apes* remain unaltered.

With respect to the two recent "behaviorist" novels mentioned earlier, Amis makes *Lucky Jim* lead somewhere (Jim gets the girl and the job); but the comic technique of the book suffers, or rather simply disappears. *Lolita,* with its more complicated and satisfactory action, turns toward the tragic as its hero distinguishes between the Lolita of his imagination and the pregnant wife of Mr. Dick Schiller whom he visits near the end of the book. Lewis ends his novel by handing Snooty the simplest of wish-fulfillments—a cute little mistress—perhaps to indicate how little the author cared about what happened to his hero. By pumping the novel full of what, in an earlier reference to Humph, was derogatorily termed "the false pep of action," an absurd solution is provided to Snooty's very unbehavioristic, existentialist questionings in front of the hatter's dummy. It is dangerous and probably unconvincing to try to work out any firm line of interpretation for so wayward a book—to make it lead anywhere—yet in one important way the novel hints of those to come as much as, for all Kenner's tracing of its affiliations with the earlier fiction, it is the novelist's last gesture in a blind alley.

Positively, *Snooty* is the first of Lewis' novels to achieve an expression of the polemicist's critical and colloquial irony within the novel form, even if the form is in this case relatively feeble. Sometimes the "coarsening" of voice is merely a crude inverting of idealism—Jamesian or Virginia Woolfian; Snooty sighs "Oh Listerine!" as he attacks his mistress who suffers from halitosis. As the cliché goes, nothing is sacred to the narrator; even his own iconoclasm and debunking are subjected to the same morose boredom he directs at others. Concomitantly, and more significantly, the debunking extends to the whole idea of the novel as a dramatic representation of significant human action. The conspiracy between Lewis and the knowing reader has no respect for, or even belief in, the possible refinements of the novel form. It should be remembered that Lewis at about this time was praising Hemingway for writing, with considerable artistry, novels of violent action. Lewis' first attempt at the proletarizing or coarsening of his own novelistic style gives us a hero contemptuous of any such artists, and for the moment an author who sympathizes with him, perhaps more than he consciously realized.[5]

Although the five years between *Snooty* and *The Revenge for Love* show no published novels, Lewis did complete and see into proofs the short and suppressed *The Roaring Queen* (1936). Reading the book is a mildly depressing experience; it is, among other things, a satire on the book-reviewing racket, but it contains nothing that had not already been done with more life in *Apes* and in *Snooty*. Lewis seems bored by his subject, even when it broadens to include a young miss named Baby Bucktrout who carries around a copy of *Lady Chatterley's Lover* and who unsuccessfully attempts to force an un-Mellors-like rustic named Tom to do her will. After Lewis' own insistence two years before in *Men Without Art* that fiction-satire-art must preoccupy itself with the disasters of the peace, he produced a book which studiously averts its gaze from any but the most familiar and literary sights; even the sympathetic reader must feel that Arnold Bennett book-puffery or schoolgirl versions of Lawrentian doctrine are by no means the significant disasters of the mid-1930's.

It would be imaginatively right if, as Hugh Kenner suggests, the sight of *The Roaring Queen* in proofs was such a dreadful experience that Lewis immediately had it withdrawn; but it is evident from one of the letters that his publishers were worried about the possible libel on "real people"—though few characters seem less real than these. In any case, Kenner is perfectly right to say that suddenly "the incalculable happened" and that in the troubled years to come Lewis produced his best novels and pictures. In the first of these, *The Revenge for Love*, the achievement is most substantial and most surprising. While this novel incorporates, as much as is necessary for its purposes, the colloquial irony and wit of *Snooty*, they are made use of within a purposeful development. The book's strong artistry refutes the possibility— hinted at in *Snooty* and confirmed by the ill-fated *Roaring Queen* —that novels in the dreary 1930's could only be writen by fools or wise guys for the consumption of fools and cynics.

II   The Revenge for Love

In *The Revenge for Love* what seems for the first hundred or so pages a rambling introduction of various unrelated figures, eventually turns into a book with no loose ends and with all careers and issues resolved. Even a cursory account of events may suggest its organic nature. Divided into seven parts, it opens in a Spanish prison and traces the attempted escape, shooting, and subsequent recovery in the hospital of Percy Hardcaster, a fat communist agitator from the working classes who returns to England minus a leg but with a legendary status as a martyr to fascism. Part Two introduces the failed artist, Victor Stamp, who contemplates the gas oven but is cared for faithfully by his devoted wife, Margot. In a burst of unexpected energy Victor paints a passable picture and decides that the fates have not yet turned up his number. Part Three abruptly turns attention to "Jolly Jack" Cruze, a businessman whose real sport is lechery—a "bit of skirt." Jack is visited on a tax matter by Tristy Phipps, a painter and a devoted party-liner in politics; when Jack discovers that Tristy paints nudes, he is immediately thrilled and gets invited round to meet the painter's upper-class, militantly Marxist wife Gillian (later referred to as Gillian Communist), and their sad-faced crowd of leftist sympathizers. During a salute to Percy Hardcaster's sacrifice, Jack reveals his politics to be less than correct; but he decides that Gillian will be his next adventure in "skirt."

All these figures come together in Part Four at a large party thrown by Sean O'Hara, a professional member of the Third International, who is in cahoots with the unscrupulous businessman Abershaw to do some gunrunning over the Spanish border and to involve both Stamp and Percy in the action. Each character pursues his particular demon; at the same time, interrelations begin to emerge clearly during the finely rendered chaos of a convincing party. From this point on, the book focuses mainly on Victor, Margot, and Percy (who has been beaten out and beaten up by Jack Cruze in a contest for Gillian's favors—Percy has exposed the unreality of her fashionable version of communism) and on the violent culmination of their gunrunning mission in Spain. Through a complicated double-cross and a well-meaning mistake, Percy ends up in prison once more; there he receives the news of Margot's and Victor's deaths in the mountains. The book ends as he hears Margot's voice and sheds a tear.

From even this truncated version of events, the book looks as if it could pass for a *bona fide* novel of action, and indeed it does. There are moments toward the end—particularly when Victor runs down a Spanish civil guard, then continues to hurtle on in the auto with the numbed Margot at his side—when, although a strong style is controlling our responses, we read simply to find out what happens next. The only thing in Lewis' previous work comparable to these final headlong chapters is Otto Kreisler's flight to death in *Tarr*, but that, by comparison, seems labored and remote. Yet at the same time, we hardly read with our fingers crossed in hopes that the lovers will make it back across the French border; the episode cannot be confused with simple narrative suspense like the lovers' escape to Switzerland in Hemingway's *A Farewell to Arms*, for Margot's (and Lewis') voice gives meaning to the events. These meanings are independent of whatever in particular happens next, and are such that an escape in the nick of time, followed by wipings of the brow and a resolve henceforth to stay out of danger, would be ludicrous and impossible. In short, *The Revenge for Love* is a novel of action that is also "about" action in a way the simple novel of action cannot be; and the rich adequacy of its "coarse" style turns the book about life into a complex experience rather than a lecture.

The opening is theatrically arresting:

"Claro," said the warder. "Claro, hombre!" It was the condescension
of one caballero to another. His husky voice was modulated upon the
principle of an omniscient rationality. When he spoke, he spoke from
the bleak socratic peak of his wisdom to another neighbouring peak—
equally equipped with the spotless panoply of logic. Deep answered
to deep—height hurled back its assent to height! "Claro, hombre!" he
repeated, tight-lipped, with the controlled passion of the great logician. "We are never free to choose—because we are only free once in
our lives."

"And when is that?" inquired the prisoner.

"That is when at last we gaze into the bottom of the heart of our
beloved and find that it is false—like everything else in the world!"

The thematic keynote is set (Lewis originally wanted to call the
book *False Bottoms* then prudently desisted); but, more important stylistically, the heroic-Miltonic note is established and
immediately questioned by the potential narrative insolence of
"spotless" and "great logician." Although the prisoner, Percy
Hardcaster, takes issue with the sententious pronouncements of
his captor, he is equipped as a Marxist with his own "spotless panoply of logic" which is stained by the events of the novel.

In the following passage, narrative insolence becomes broader
and more offhand as the scene comes into focus:

There were two crashes in rapid succession, a third, and then the
outbreak of demoniacal cries. The Andalusion evening shed down its
brilliant operatic light upon the just and the unjust alike. At a long
table in the center of the large concreted patio sat a dozen unjust
men. Twelve of the most unjust in Spain, at the moment. They were
unsuccessful politicos. They had been caught red-handed, with arms
in their hands. . . . Their furious shouts, harshened by extreme ca-
tarrh, as they crashed Joker and King down upon the table, alarmed
the pigeons patrolling the skyline of Baltic-Blue over their heads—
who made themselves into perambulating fans, to receive the coolness
of the evening breezes into their overheated wing-pits, their button
eyes cocked towards the remote sierra, from whence the coolness came
in irregular bursts of gently-flowing air.

(1–2)

Since the Spaniards are deliberating whether to find the prisoners
innocent or guilty when they come to trial and whether they

should receive the firing squad or a "magnificent Spanish pardon," the rich cadence of "the just and the unjust" rings as sententiously irrelevant to the situation as does Don Alvaro's spotless logic; so the narrator's casual tip that they were "Twelve of the most unjust in Spain, at the moment" indicates awareness of the irrelevance.

The operatic light promises to be a comic one, and genial Shavian scene-setting prevails until the prose abruptly evokes an alarmed nature, grandly described through the birds. This image establishes one of the principal relationships of the book—that of human violence set in opposition to the potentially undisturbed and heedless nature surrounding it. The narrator sees around the thrilling solemnity of either logic or melodramatic action, even to the lengths of insinuating the first of many puns about "reds" ("red-handed," "red-blooded"). At the same time, the elegant care with which the pigeons are poised suggests that a metaphorically thickened prose can be more than the object of parody or mockery it was in *Snooty Baronet:* Andalusian nature is accorded an authentic reality instead of being contemptuously tossed aside to make way for aggressive Behaviorists. Perhaps the operatic note will not be purely comic after all. The troubled breadth of scene is something new in Lewis' fiction (except in the fantastic sense such breadth assumes in *Childermass*) and indicates a corresponding widening in subject and in narrative spirit.

The surprise of the book is Margot Stamp, who is created by means of a style that has nothing in common with any to be found in Lewis' other books. She is introduced unglamorously, upon awaking, as she watches her sleeping husband Victor and meditates on the unluckiness of love, and on its powerlessness against events and death that takes revenge on it for being love. Margot sobs; then, while gazing at Victor, she is described thus:

Her head of a small wistful seabird, delicately drafted to sail in the eye of the wind, and to skate upon the marbled surface of the waves —with its sleek feathery chevelure, in long matted wisps—arched downward on its neck to observe Lord Victor. The rhythm of his heaves, in his sulky imposture of sleep, certainly approximated to the ocean. She hovered over him in her ecstasy of lovesickness, her eyes full of a dizzy gloating, rocked by the steady surge of his chest. Her eyes were almost popping out of her skull in the intensity of her desire *to settle*—to skim down and settle: to ride there and to be at rest!

(66–67)

What would have been occasion for manic laughter in *The Apes of God* is no longer such. The narrative names the pose harshly enough—"an ecstasy of lovesickness"—but, as the metaphor develops, indulgences are made graceful and dignified. Later in the section Victor suddenly awakes "stabbed with the sensation of her uneasy care"; then he muses on Margot's solicitude and his own response to it: "Not to let down another creature, who had brought her life over and cast in her lot with yours, what sort of fool's dream was that? But maybe it was a question of good luck, if nothing more; just as you would not willingly betray the trustfulness of a bird that makes its nest against your window. A rugged unrevolutionary principle, founded upon sentiment, not intellect" (77).

The relation of this passage to the opening section's doctrinaire histrionics begins to emerge; if the rugged unrevolutionary principle of sentiment that holds the lovers together smacks of Arnold's "Dover Beach," there is room for more than pathos in the style:

"But we're all right, Victor—we'll get over the present, you know we shall: things *are* sticky, as you'd call it, now, darling, I know. Just *now*."

"Ay—take the good times with the bad!" he jeered.

She began crying, with little soft pants, into a pocket handkerchief. His jaw softened its lines. A mellower light was seen in his eyes. He reached over and hooked her towards him; dragging the small weeping creature up against his chest—reared up upon the edge of the bed, rampant as a figure in a frieze, all in the two dimensions.

(74)

There is nothing startling about this bit of looking back in anger or sorrow, yet the verb "hooked" and the formality of the two-dimensional frieze turn pathos—even modified by sarcasm—into something original, something beyond the possibilities of mere stage dialogue or true romance.

In the first section of the book, revolutionary heroics and public betrayals are seasoned with mockery. Then, with the introduction of Margot and Victor, unrevolutionary sentiment and private loyalties are broadly portrayed, but formalized and raised to resilient authenticity. There remains a third stylistic strain in the novel—that in which Jack Cruze lives, moves, and has his being. He was, when younger, a true son of Tom Jones, as the juicy Fielding-

esque narrative reminds us: "seeking out the shy short-skirted fil-
lies and tiny flappers, and bringing blushes to many a small dim-
pled cheek with his unbecoming remarks and enterprising habits.
With the older girls he disappeared into shrubberies, from which
astonished squeals would issue. Everyone soon knew, for miles
around, what Master Jackie Cruze was like" (92). As the narration of Jack's career proceeds and chapters begin with "Well" or
"Well I've said," the style relaxes and broadens to a point where it
looks as if the novel can hardly accommodate it. But coarseness of
narration, unlike its situation in *Snooty Baronet,* has something
more dignified to play itself off against; thus it never gains control
of the novel, though it is never totally absent even after Jack
Cruze leaves the scene for good.

Jack is what Lewis has referred to as a "sex-nuisance"; but,
rather than figuring as the object of easy satire, he is used in this
organic book as an unwitting agency for exposing the pious, hu-
morless Red circle that surrounds Gillian and Tristy and that
spends evenings brooding about capitalist-fascist treacheries:
"this was a pretty grisly lot of dismal Jimmies. About that there
were no two ways, thought this great keen-eyed kid from the
outer darkness. There they sat or sprawled, sucking their old pipes
and egging each other on as it seemed to the astonished outsider,
to give each other the blues" (105–6). The chipper, roughhouse
idiom is continuous with "Master Jackie" even down to calling the
pipes "old"; and later on Jack is indeed a bad boy, interrupting a
conversation about Spain to tell the story of a business pal who
had been arrested, robbed, and thrown into jail. When one of the
faithful, hoping to add to his stock of fascist atrocity stories asks
whether it happened in Valencia, Jack replies innocently "No that
wasn't it . . . What do they call it now? Petrograd. Yes, that's
right! Petrograd. He said *the pauperism*—it had to be seen to be
believed" (109).

By using such a "sport" to bring out the rigidities and simplici-
ties of fashionable fellow traveling, the novel's political bias is less
rigid than when the narrator steps in on his own with resolution to
be a roving satirist. For, since no one but Jack and Percy Hardcaster himself can expose the falsities of these romantic revolutionaries (Margot and Victor are preoccupied, withdrawn until
the end), there are moments when Wyndham Lewis appears too
recognizably as The Enemy and sets up a character only to mas-

sacre him: "A 'Leftie' reporter had out his note-book, and he had noted that Hardcaster, the English syndicalist, had been put in a cell window which looked out upon a swamp, and there had been left practically to his own devices for three days and three nights . . . and that the nursing sisters—wrongly supposing him to be unconscious had rubbed salt into his sores" (149). The point gets made, but its abstract externality of presentation shows that the material has not been worked into the novel's life. That such moments are infrequent is a tribute to Lewis' dramatic sense and to his willingness to complicate his own (at that moment) rightist politics.

This complication is mainly seen in the portrayal of Percy Hardcaster. Nothing in the "anti-war" books (*Left Wings* and *Count Your Dead*) that are contemporary with the novel suggests that Lewis could imagine a communist with anything but the most reductive contempt and ridicule. Yet, compared to the "parlor pinks" who eagerly devour the trumped-up story of Percy's heroics, Percy emerges as a disenchanted realist to whom eventually a personal voice can speak and be heard. He acknowledges that he lives in a world of men without art where it is perfectly natural for a one-legged and disabled person like himself to be knocked down and kicked by a sex rival like Jack Cruze. Even his self-righteous insistence on the logicality of events is brought into question by the end of the book. When Tristy visits him in the hospital after his beating and exclaims: "Why, you are a different person! What for? What was it for?" the answer he gets is "For nothing"; and the narrator explicates this by speaking of "the nothingness at the heart of the most plausible and pretentious of affirmatives, either as man or as thing" (272). The world, the main image of the novel indicates, is a false bottom; and this discovery should lead at least to the eschewal of heroics.

Lewis' own politics during the 1930's were predicated on this discovery. The limitations of his "anti-war" books can be better understood if we note that, while *The Art of Being Ruled* is filled with flashes of brilliant, speculative politics, and while even *Hitler* is in part a work of political theory, *Left Wings* and *Count Your Dead* are quite unspeculative; they are preoccupied instead with exposing the nothingness of various "plausible and pretentious affirmatives" being proclaimed in the years 1935–37. As both consequence and cause of this practical criticism, Wyndham Lewis became and remained, to most intellectuals, a name indentified with barbarous, inhuman political beliefs; and many who doubtless had failed to work their way through *The Art of Being Ruled* were quick to condemn the crude heresies he now espoused.

Julian Symons in his short survey *The Thirties* points out that, unlike T. S. Eliot who by this time was fully accepted as an "eccentric reactionary" whose opinions really didn't matter much because he had written such important poetry, Lewis, along with George Orwell, assumed the character of a *memento mori:* " 'If we were not as we are, if we had not been saved, this,' orthodox Artists and Pragmatists thought with a shiver as they contemplated the Fascist monster Lewis and the Trotskyist demon Orwell, 'is what we might have become.' " [6] Symons adds that, at one point, the Left Book Club groups were seriously considering boycotting Lewis' works; and Orwell himself testifies to the instant political redefinition that intellectuals engaged in:

> If there was one thing that the British intelligentsia were committed to, it was the debunking version of war, the theory that war is all corpses and latrines and never leads to any good result. Well, the same people who in 1933 sniggered pityingly if you said that in certain circumstances you would fight for your country, in 1937 were denouncing you as a Trotsky-Fascist if you suggested that the stories in New Masses about freshly wounded men clamouring to get back into the fighting might be exaggerated. And the Left intelligentsia made their swing-over from "War is hell" to "War is glorious" not only with no sense of incongruity but almost without any intervening stage.[7]

It is probably also true that Lewis began to enjoy his romantic Enemy role of being what Auden called, in a fine phrase, "That lonely old volcano of the Right." [8] This relish did not add to the objectivity of his political criticism. While he displays an excellent eye in the "anti-war" books for exposing the nothingness of affirmations by Maxim Litvinov or Stanley Baldwin, or the dangers of alliances on the part of England and France with the interests of Soviet Russia, this eye glazes over as it looks at Franco's Spain or at Hitler's Germany. The satirist is not complete enough; the ideal *clerc* has become engaged in debunking one side and has lost his powers of providing equal treatment for the other. In this respect Orwell emerges as a more satisfactory political journalist, since the inclusiveness of his work is superior to that of his fellow heretic.

Insofar as the political satire in *The Revenge for Love* is pretty much confined to the Left, Lewis' novel is also less than inclusive; but this lack is much less important since he is in good company—with James and Conrad that is, rather than with British fascists of the 1930's. James's *The Princess Cassamassima* and Conrad's *The Secret Agent* both treat revolutionaries as foolish or misguided; but, more importantly, they dramatize what these movements cost in human lives, especially those of people who become involved with politics through no clear will or choice of their own. James's Hyacinth Robinson and Conrad's Winnie Verloc are not models for Victor and Margot Stamp, but neither of them is a revolutionary hero. In the "conservative" novels of their authors, some "rugged unrevolutionary principle" guides Hyacinth and Winnie to suicide or murder; and at these moments their selfhood is affirmed and annihilated.

The Revenge for Love, like these predecessors, is a novel of action that is "about" action as well, or rather about the representations of actions that literature—English literature in particular—has offered the human spirit. The most magnificent representations were offered by Shakespeare, whose example is important in Lewis' work as a whole and especially in the makeup of this, his best novel. In *The Lion and the Fox* published ten years before, Lewis argued for a "personal" Shakespeare who, in an age profoundly interested and influenced by Machiavelli, provided the richest criticisms of the life of action. Machiavelli figures for Lewis as a great writer who could imagine no kind of life but a political one and who was, consequently, a theoretician of action—of "the acquisition and exercise of authority over other men." Machiavelli's doctrine has great force and simplicity in its pursuit of these techniques; but interestingly he, along with later devotees of action like Rousseau and Stendhal, was markedly ineffective in his own life. Lewis concludes that:

It seems to be that the qualities that make a man a successful theoretician are the opposite to those that make him a successful man of action: and that even if, as in the case of Machiavelli, he is a theoretician of *action*. The material of which the mirror destined to reflect action is made is at the other pole to the violent ferments providing the substance of *action*. Perhaps, as the *reflecting* mind is at all events living, it would be better to say that it must be both motionless and deep to reflect to the fullest advantage the conflict occurring in the world.

(*The Lion and the Fox*, 186)

The mind, above all others, most motionless and deep in English or perhaps any literature was Shakespeare's. He is the accommodating artist, a "particularly glorious parasite on everything"; and his supposed impersonality is not a birthright but a hard-won mask. Lewis is determinedly old-fashioned in emphasizing once more the great-souled Shakespeare—of Bradley and the Romantics—who wrote tragedies about the falls of heroic men of action. The "grand and mournful rhetoric" given these figures at their moments of high utterance shows that in falling into abjectness, they become great, failed heroes. And in these instances, Lewis argues, we enter the region of Shakespeare's truest, most imaginative allegiances.

Although at certain moments in *The Lion and the Fox* Lewis seems bent on outdoing Lamb or Swinburne in admiring Shakespeare's heroes (". . . all splendid masterpieces, all reproducing the same music of extinction and unbounded suffering. They are a gallery of sunsets: they are dream-storms in a single soul . . ." [290]), he is also at pains to insist that those heroes are pathetic children, conventional and mechanical, sometimes unattractive (Coriolanus is wonderfully described as, apart from his warlike feats, a "glum, vain and extremely peevish dog" [241])—and that all of them are "monsters of grandeur and simplicity." Hamlet becomes then, in his inaction, not a typical Shakespearean tragic hero but the embodiment in a play of a "system of predilections and beliefs"; tragic art in general is termed "the enemy of human energy and success, or such a check on them as to be that, and the opponent of action" (170). Ten years later Lewis wrote *The Revenge for Love*, a novel in which satire turns toward the tragic. Shakespearean heroics become especially relevant when we consider the two individuals, Victor and Margot, who stand at the heart of the book.

Victor, the simpler figure, is presented at first from the inside as he paints a decent picture and decides Fate hasn't yet turned up his number. As the novel proceeds, this relative psychological complication is eliminated; from without, Victor Stamp equals various masks worn, as far as we can see, without interest or feeling: a Clark Gable smile, a Vincent Van Gogh who is forging self-portraits, a Gun-Running Decoy whose cargo is actually a load of bricks and who remains oblivious to the dangers of his situation. What look like gestures of individual freedom, most obviously the stamping-on of his forged Van Gogh, are made with no accompanying analysis or deliberation of motive. The instinctual has its affinities with the mechanical; and the fortunes of such a wild body—an "aimless thing" as Margot calls him—is an old Lewisian theme; but the progressive narrowing of Victor from a person to a thing seems natural instead of arbitrary because he is seen mainly through the intense and sympathetic eyes of Margot.

If we speculate as to the look of a twentieth-century tragedy, written in the livest form available—the novel, set off by the "disasters of the peace" and coarsened in accordance—*The Revenge for Love* is a conceivable outcome. Antony or Coriolanus, in the dress of 1937, becomes a he-mannish movie star, a wild Australian man of action who, like the Hemingway hero, has only rudimentary words for his situation and is in the ranks of those to whom things happen. Like Shakespeare's heroes, Victor is a child, even a "monster of grandeur and simplicity" in the Hollywood sense suggested by the clichés that describe him. Or Victor can be seen as an Antony deprived of the Shakespearean use of words but, like Antony, ruined and ennobled by the woman who would have him for herself. Or, like Coriolanus, refusing to accept the language of others as definitive of himself, Victor is the modern maverick-individual-artist (however second-rate) whose identity in the collectivist world of men without art must be wiped out.

These connections are not fanciful since the characters themselves try to turn Victor into something comprehensible. As Margot's consciousness becomes, under various pressures, fantastic and allegorical, she sees him as a symbolic lion who is "it" and doesn't know it, whose day as the king of beasts has passed. Lewis, like the heroine of his novel and in her words, most surely finds himself "in the camp of the defeated Victors"; the identification with Shakespeare, conscious or unconscious as it may have been for him in 1937, asserts itself in terms similar to those used in *The Lion and the Fox* about Shakespeare's allegiances to his "great failed heroes."

But to have allegiances to a hero does not insure any worth to the novel about his fortunes. The problem of working out an acceptable relationship between narrator and hero that will be neither sentimental nor, in Lewis' more accustomed way, crisply detached, cannot be solved in *Snooty Baronet* fashion by substituting third for first-person narration. It would not make very much difference, that is, if the close of *A Farewell to Arms* about the "I" going out into the rain were about a "he" instead. The particular genius of *The Revenge for Love* is that Lewis avoids a direct relation with his failed, heroic man of action and presents him instead through the voice of Margot as she moves through growing concern about Victor to madness and death.

The penultimate section of the novel is titled "The Fakers"; and, though the reference is most obviously to Victor and Tristy's efforts in the fake factory at "increasing the number of Van Goghs in the world," there are other chapters in which more subtle fakery takes place. This section opens with Margot awaiting the arrival of a feminist friend in the latter's room. The room borders on a park, termed by the narrator a "well of beautiful loneliness"; Margot imagines herself lying under one of its elms, book in hand: "And as she idly considered what book she should take down with her, if this were *her* room, to read in that exquisite seclusion of this heaven-sent deep bit of park (thrown away on barbarians like Agnes), she thought that *A Room of One's Own* would exactly suit the requirements of the case—would beautifully abet the lonely occasion" (229).

Despite the reminiscences of the attack on Virginia Woolf in *Men Without Art,* she and her "feminist tract" are only one of a number of literary references and figures that combine in Margot's idealized version of herself in the what-might-have-been. Both Virginia Woolf in *A Room of One's Own* and Ruskin in *Sesame and Lilies* quote lines from Tennyson's "Maud" at crucial moments; so Margot, adjusting the words to her own situation, raptly chants, "I am coming my own, my sweet! / I am coming my love, my dear!":

Her lips uttered, with scarcely more than a phantom of sound, the romantic declaration. And the words, so diaphanously winged, passed out into the haunted air of the unexpected park—where, at any moment, the solitude might be invaded, and heightened, by two figures who, at a likely guess, if you followed them to discover their habitat, would reintegrate the pages of Framley Parsonage, but *never* derive from anything more grossly twentieth-century or anything privy to internal combustion—to name the arch-serpent of the pre-war Eden. "*What poets they were!*" she repeated to herself, in the very words of Virginia Woolf. "*What poets they were!*" *They* being those splendid Victorian monogamists—flowering, as great-hearted passion flowers, hyperpetalous and crimson red, upon the spoils of the Anglo-Indies and of the Dark Continent.

(231–32)

Although the spell is broken by the "brazen" anti-romantic entrance of the New Woman, Agnes Irons, it evokes magnificently the self-styled "hermit girl" and the kind of reading which provided her sustenance. Taken together, this reading promised her a room of her own that Margot now occupies only in rare moments of privileged theft such as the present. The fakery of these writers, who lead the unwary to identify reality with their glossy literary versions of it, is largely a matter of the high tone, whether in the singing Tennyson, the pontificating Ruskin, or the divinely thrilling Virginia ("What poets they were!"); and perhaps Margot is not the only one who feels the splendor and sadness of this tone. Lewis has never seemed more genially attracted, though with both eyes open, by the seductive mellowness of these well-to-do versions of experience; if he doesn't share his heroine's wistfulness toward them, he does imagine them with energetic fascination.

But, if the revenge for love is death, the revenge for being taken in by these noble and heady sentiments is no less sharp. So Margot realizes in the final section of the book in which two juxtaposed incidents point her developing sense of things—not, crudely, toward reality away from romance, but from a romantic view of things to one that is wilder and harsher. In other words, she moves closer in knowledge and sympathies to the most inclusive consciousness in the novel—that of Wyndham Lewis, the narrator. In the first of these chapters, the insistent attention of a dwarf who shrieks at her from outside a Spanish café indicates (despite Victor's confident disclaimers) that there is no escape—no room of one's own away from "the roaring and spluttering bestial life of flash and blood" (295).

In the succeeding episode, she lies near a mountain stream and realizes that nature, far from presenting the literary Wordsworthian perfection she had been brought up to admire, offers instead only "a senseless agitation of unfeeling things." With an exclamation she reserves her right to remain outside this nature since she is part of the agony of men, since "It was Victor who was her *nature* now; and 'wild nature' too, at that" (305). Then she thinks of Ruskin's impassioned address to women—the "lilies" of *Sesame and Lilies;* back come the words of Virginia Woolf and the lines from Tennyson, but they only depress her. With Victor as her nature, she rejects Ruskin's "sweeping belittlement of the male" and also his inspiring flattery of women as "Queens." Or she will permit herself to identify only with the Shakespearean woman who, in Ruskin's account, failed her mate at a crucial time; if she cannot move Victor out of this false bottom, this bag of tricks he is caught up in, then she can ironically qualify for the Ophelia role —that of the "Incompetent Mate." With an abrupt gesture, she leaves Ruskin by the brook and rejoins the world.

In both instances Margot's responses have become extravagant and symbolical. She reads behind the lines of the book of nature, or of art; she constructs meanings that are a torment rather than a comfort to her spirit; and that torment is a measure of their reality. The pitch is reached as she and Victor run down the civil guard and hurtle on ever faster to oblivion; appropriately, her inner narrative speeds up, collapses, and assimilates objects into one another with widening brilliance. To apply Lewis' own language about Shakespeare's heroes, as Margot becomes mad she becomes a philosopher (we don't ask which precedes which); and her readings of events take on the final sweep of passionate accounting.

In this culminating paragraph the claims of romance, of feminine pathetic fallacies, combine astonishingly with a harsher spirit, a coarser language, to enhance rather than cancel out each other. Margot has called Victor a hero—the symbol of a life that is passed: "How much she loved this aimless thing! But she was Nature mourning for the mate of her youth. She was the wind sighing on the wart-leaves for its existence among the glacial peaks, after a levelling of all the splendid mountains. She was the sigh of the last rose, and the whisper of the last lily, when the Flower-haters have decreed the extinction of all 'luxury-weeds.'" And, though Tennyson and Ruskin have invited her as Maud or Magdalen to come into the garden where, it may be, He, the

Gardener, will welcome her as woman and Queen, she finds she
has rewritten the poem:

So, and in that symbolical manner, she could respond to the song of
the magdalen, brought to her notice by the latter-day wolves, who
had suckled her starved intelligence and fed it with Victorian lollypops.

> *The red rose cries, 'He is near, he is near,'*
> *And the white rose weeps, 'He is late';*
> *The larkspur listens, 'I hear, I hear,'*
> *And the lily whispers, 'I wait.'*

(356)

The fineness of this passage lies in its recognition and admission
of irony and love as the two strongest assertions of an individual
response to nature, to the world of action, to chaos. The words
carry their symbolic burden without apology; the metaphors are
more than flashy gestures thrown up by a posturing narrator. As
with the passage, so with the novel taken as a whole. Lewis' stylistic and moral triumph consists of his narrative combination of
irony and love against whatever system threatens individual reality in the name of action: Marxism, Heroic Victorianism, or any
number of other systems and guides to conduct—either the accredited mythologies of the past, or the ideological world of the
present and future.

The novel is in defense of the individual voice and its asserted
humanness, although that voice will be no more successful in prevailing against the March of Events than were any of Lewis' own
books in the 1930's. Yet, if articulated by the novelist, the voice
may be heard by another person, momentarily made individual
himself in an unaccustomed experience. This happens at the close
of the novel when Percy Hardcaster is brought the news of Margot and Victor's deaths. Sulking in prison, he continues his
Marxist-agent pose as "The Injured Party":

But meanwhile a strained and hollow voice, part of a sham-culture
outfit, but tender and halting, as if dismayed at the sound of its own
bitter words, was talking in his ears, in a reproachful singsong. It was
denouncing him out of the past, where alone now it was able to articulate; it was singling him out as a man who led people into mortal danger, people who were dear beyond expression to the possessor of the

passionate, the artificial, the unreal, yet penetrating, voice, and crying to him now to give back, she implored him, the young man, Absalom, whose life he had had in his keeping, and who had somehow,
unaccountably, been lost, out of the world and out of Time!

(377)

That the novel sustains and justifies, even to the syntactical difficulties, this very untypical Lewisian rhetorical flight, is proof of
the weight endowed in the individual voice of Margot Stamp; at
the same time the formal, generalizing style in its dignified lamentation accords scope to individual tragedy. Percy, in a gesture that
Lewis calls self-pity, drops a tear on the floor; but, no matter how
the motive is named, the voice has been heard.

The most fitting irony that followed upon publication of *The
Revenge for Love* was *Partisan Review*'s refusal to print a laudatory review of the novel by Rebecca Citkovitch.[9] The refusal confirmed Lewis' sense that everything, novels very much included,
was judged by its politics. Thirty years later, although the book
has received generous praise and consideration from a number of
writers, it remains largely unknown while André Malraux's *Man's
Fate*, which in comparison looks like the work of a Minister of
Culture, passes as the authentic political novel.

III   The Vulgar Streak

Lewis' final "novel of the 1930's"—*The Vulgar Streak*—was actually completed in the summer of 1940 on Long Island, and published in England in September 1941. By that time he was established in the dismal Hotel Tudor in Toronto which would receive
its own literary immortality in a future novel. But *The Vulgar
Streak* looks backward on a society, indeed a world, whose like
will not be seen again. Lewis' smallest, most economical, and most
schematic piece of fiction, the novel demands not so much explication—its outlines present themselves clearly—as an articulated
impression of its peculiar strength and modesty, a quality we do
not expect to encounter in a novel by Wyndham Lewis. Its presence in this one is dependent on an almost total effacement of the
author's personality. Compared to *Tarr* or to *The Apes of God*,
The Revenge for Love is a chaste book; yet it contains narrative
high-jinks (the Jack Cruze sections), various kinds of mock-heroic

(Hardcaster and the Spaniards), and a rhetorically heightened impressionism through which Margot asserts herself. On the other hand, *The Vulgar Streak* is all of a piece; sober or ironic by turn, it never raises its voice to hector or cajole.

Perhaps for this very reason Lewis feared that the point of the novel might be missed—the letters of this period contain a number of accounts of his intentions in writing the book. One of these —the first draft of a letter to H. G. Wells, and thoughtfully included by Mr. Rose—puts the book's hero, Vincent Penhale, in the tradition of Stendahl's Julien Sorel and Dostoyevsky's Raskolnikoff—themselves disciples of the "ruthless" tradition of Napoleonic action—with this explanation:

It seemed to me that the time had come to add another book to this line . . . it seemed to me that this doctrine taken over by Hitler, and influencing so many minds in Europe, might be made to do its fell work in the soul of a character in fiction, once again. On very different lines, it was time to project another Sorel or Raskolnikoff; whose bug would not be the Napoleonic bug this time, but rather the self-conscious "power," "force," and "action" that has infected so many people today . . . at the same time I would strike a blow against the class-nonsense, that weakens us in England so much.

(*L*, 332)

And as, on the eve of his suicide, the hero enjoys a last supper with his sidekick, Martin Penny-Smythe, the same identifications are brought out in conversation.

The novel begins in Venice and traces Vincent Penhale's courtship and conquest of Miss April Mallow against the backdrop of exchanges between Hitler and Neville Chamberlain. War breaks out, the characters return to London, and Vincent—having successfully concealed his lower-class origins from April—pursues his "business." The business is a public analogue to his private couterfeiting: he is engaged in the making and passing of false money. When the authorities catch up with his public counterfeiting, Vincent signals the end of his private show as well by hanging himself.

In an obvious way the thematic "meaning" of the book is perfectly clear and comes as no surprise to a reader of *The Revenge for Love* and of Lewis' other books. Yet his insistent underlining of this theme should not obscure the character of the novel from which it is abstracted. *The Vulgar Streak,* compared to Stendhal's *The Red and the Black* or Dostoyevsky's *Crime and Punishment,* lacks the intense analytical presence of an author concerned with exploring his hero's behavior; indeed, the effacement of Lewis is complete enough to make the book seem spare and unruminative in accordance with Vincent Penhale's confession that he is "all action." Unlike Lewis' other novels, it does not lend itself to nor demand very much quotation to illustrate its nature. There is no narrator who, as at the end of *The Revenge for Love,* cries out in high style about "the young man, Absalom." On the contrary, Vincent, who bears many resemblances to Victor Stamp, from his aggressive-sounding name to his Clark Gable looks, writes his own epitaph in the terse note found pinned to his chest: "Whoever wants this body, may do what they like with it. I don't want it. *Signed.* Its former inhabitant" (240).

Thinking back to *Tarr,* and remembering the similar fate of Otto Kreisler, we note the enormous difference in how the narrative treats these two men-of-action; for, when Lewis called the death of Kreisler a "mechanical tragedy," he was pointing at an action significantly distinct from the death that concludes *The Vulgar Streak.* It is not profitable to argue about whether a given hero in a Lewis novel is or is not a partial "self-portrait" of the author; all of them are; but, unlike Kreisler, Vincent Penhale is allowed a final expression of sentiments and knowledge that moves him near the voice of Wyndham Lewis. In the final pages of the book Vincent confronts the fact that his reckless counterfeit game has introduced chaos into the lives of others: his wife, his sister, his mother-in-law. The terse recognition that his counterfeit "I" was but an "it"—and a most irresponsible and violent one —is the only insight gained from the tragedy, and is absolutely sufficient; in the act of suicide Vincent disowns the sham of his own past without atoning in any way for the human cost to others.

Concentration on the "theme" of the novel leaves out its extraordinarily resourceful rendering of manners and speech. There are scenes, especially that of the funeral of Vincent's father, in which Lewis convinces us that he could have been a fully accredited master of the comedy of manners if other concerns had not so frequently interfered. As Vincent's father is about to be buried, his mother realizes that her husband "don't got 'is teeth in." Rectifying this situation falls to brother Harry, who approaches the disdainful Vincent:

"Half a mo. Wot is we to do, Vin, about . . . ?" He came nearer and lowered his voice. "Wot about dad's teeth? Eh?"

Vincent shrugged.

"You can put them in, Harry, if you think it's really necessary."

It was a new idea to Harry that it would devolve upon *him* to insert the dentures in his dead father's mouth. Vincent was footing the bill for the funeral, so it seemed *his* show. He became distinctly less interested in the matter at once.

"Well, Vin, it's as you say."

"Not at all, Harry. It's as much to do with you as it is with me. You are senior to me. If you really think . . . "

"No, old man, it's only wot Mother thought . . . "

(122–23)

The passage is not "satire" unless, as with Lewis' broadest usage, satire is made simply equivalent to art; for the novelist's relationship to life is so flexible and various that it resists sternly generic labels. Lewis thought of the action of *The Vulgar Streak* as tragic, but it is also riddled with the comic, verging on grotesque. Vincent Penhale leaves not only the aforementioned suicide note but also a frank letter of recommendation for his servile butler in which it is confided that the servant's feet smell like decaying flowers. And, though the penultimate chapter ends in the tragic vein with a piercing cry from Vincent's sister as she learns the news of his suicide, there is a short conclusion, added almost willfully it seems, in which with a mild comic acceptance the action moves back toward life.

Although in writing the novel Lewis was no doubt sincerely annoyed at the practical effects of Class Structure, the theoretical components of which he had analyzed years before in *The Art of Being Ruled*, the book cannot be read as a socially engaged tract. For one thing, while Vincent is given a number of sturdy speeches assaulting the oppressive nuisance of these barriers, his own counterfeit self limits the authority of what is called his "classy humanitarian invective." But more deeply, Vincent's final realization (which Lewis seems fully to approve) is that he has been too much the actor—there is some elaborate punning on the words "action," "acting," "actor"—and not enough the artist. Since the artist is classless, a preoccupation with humanitarian concerns cannot be his main task; thus the emphasis on Vincent's enlightenment at least partially undercuts the "classy" invectives he indulges in earlier. What remains firm is the novelist's achieved sympathy—a creative one—with the Penhale clan that is, without the spreading-on of thick "warm" local color, so outrageously itself.

A similar creativity is to be found in Lewis' renderings of various spirits of places in the novel. We begin with the about-to-be abandoned Venice of 1939, still Guardi's Venice to Vincent's eyes, still sinister underneath its glittering waterways. Then we move to the long Thames-side apartment Vincent rents for himself and April, where the illusion is that one can live securely above the "oily tide" of the human waterway; then to Hanwell Cemetery in West London where Vincent's father is lowered into a waterlogged pit at the religious climax of the burial service as the minister speaks: "Dust to the Dust! he declaimed, and taking up a lump of mud—there was nothing else in sight—let it fall in the pit and it could be heard to smack the wood of the coffin" (128–29). Finally, there is the atmosphere of Vincent's last supper with Martin Penny-Smythe—"The cold meal of canned foods; the gloom of the large pillared room; the great futile easel, like the skeleton of a pre-historic bird, stuck up in the half-lit backgrounds bare of furniture, projecting its menacing shadow" (227)—the gloom of which is only momentarily relieved by the sudden appearance of a bottle of Armagnac.

These images and places are handled with a superbly unassertive tact that is characteristic of the overall tone of *The Vulgar Streak*. By comparison, the easily more brilliant *Revenge for Love* appears to have been written at high pitch, and I think it undeniable that *The Vulgar Streak* takes on a good deal of its disenchanted gravity and humor from the circumstances Lewis found himself in as he finished the book in Sag Harbor, Long Island, his temporary home through a friend's kindness. In a strange way Vincent's sober catalogue of his past is endowed with the cast of Lewis' own musing irony as it played retrospectively about the half-century of people and places and things he had sailed away from. A letter to Sturge Moore in the following year handsomely evokes the tone with which things were confronted in some essential form as a new, necessary, but forbiddingly dismal life took shape:

How calm those days were before the epoch of wars and social revolution, when you used to sit on one side of your work-table and I on the other, and we would talk—with trees and creepers of the placid Hampstead domesticity beyond the windows, and you used to grunt with a philosophic despondence I greatly enjoyed. It was the last days of the Victorian world of artificial peacefulness—of the R.S.P.C.A. and London Bobbies, of "slumming" and Buzzards cakes. As at that time I had never heard of anything else, it seemed to my young mind in the order of nature. You—I suppose—knew it was all like the stunt of an illusionist. You taught me many things. But you never taught me *that*. I first discovered about it in 1914—with growing surprise and disgust.

(*L*, 393)

CHAPTER 7

Self Condemned: Last Will and Testaments

> For our only terra firma in a boiling and shifting world is, after all, our "self." That must cohere for us to be capable at all of behaving in any way but as mirror-images of alien realities, or as the most helpless and lowest organisms, as worms or as sponges.
>
> I have said to myself that I will fix my attention upon those things that have most meaning for me. All that seems to me to contradict or threaten those things I will do my best to modify or to defeat, and whatever I see that favours and agrees with those things I will support and do my best to strengthen.
>
> Preface to *Time and Western Man*

LIKE Pound's "Hugh Selwyn Mauberley," *The Vulgar Streak* is distinctly a farewell to England; and in Lewis' career it looked for a time most unfortunately like a distinct farewell to the novel as well. The story, mainly grim, of his life in the United States and in Canada during the years of World War II can be read in his many revealing letters from that period. Aside from personal complaint about the present, the recurring note is visionary and futuristic; indeed, the charmingly retrospective letter to Sturge Moore quoted at the end of Chapter 6 is quite untypical. Lewis, as may be remembered from a previously quoted letter to Naomi Mitchison, apologizes for the limitations of his political outlook: in the 1930's he had thought "too much about our own lot" and "too little about 'le genre humain'!"

In an attempt to remedy this oversight, his first book after World War II—*America and Cosmic Man*—replaced *Time and Western Man* with up-to-date, post-cataclysmic trappings. John Holloway in the course of an excellent analysis of Lewis' awareness of contemporary social reality points out that he does more than rail against present decay: "He knew that decay means transmutation; and perhaps the most admirable thing about his whole achievement as a man was the seemingly intense effort of concentration which he brought to apprehend and register this transmutation, even to accept it, to adapt himself to it, in spite of clear and profound revulsion." [1] Holloway, who admired the "gusto" of *America and Cosmic Man,* praises Lewis' attempt to step into the future and to tell us what he has seen.

Yet such prophecy, a heady activity, has its less exhilarating counterpart in postwar disappointment and disgust which often produce merely what one of the stories from *Rotting Hill* calls a "low-grade" pain. It is easy to note the obvious connection between low-grade maladies of the quotidian and visionary transmutations of them, but harder perhaps to see how they can combine successfully in works of imagination. The problem of giving form to these related impulses may have seemed particularly acute to the satirist watching Western man, or whatever was left of him, emerge from the wreck of World War II. Lewis, sailing home from Canada after VJ-Day, must have felt himself to be a fair enough example of the unillusioned survivor of disaster; sixty-three years old, he was no better off economically than when he had left England six years before; moreover, he was probably less than confident that, in his own phrase about Sartre, a "derelict author" would find a public. There is a moment in *The Writer and the Absolute* when Lewis, quoting V.S. Pritchett on the violent suppression of the Russian satirist Olesha, argues that the case with some qualifications might be his own—"There has been to my knowledge the same 'strange absence' of a writer's name from 'surveys,' anthologies, publishers' retrospective lists, etc." (140).

Lewis took matters into his own hands by responding in the only way he knew: between 1948 and his death in March 1957, eight books appeared—counting the two sections of *The Human Age* as one—as well as timely reprints of *Tarr, The Revenge for Love,* and *The Lion and the Fox.* Although he was working on a novel about a painter when he died, and although the final section of *The Human Age* did not get beyond the planning stage, the works that were published brought his literary career to a remarkable completion. These works are remarkable in part because almost none of the components of what had been his world of concerns for the last half-century is neglected: political analysis and prophecy; anatomy of current philosophical and artistic chic—Existentialism and Abstract Expressionism; the social and economic realities of *Rotting Hill;* further novelistic exploration of individual heroic action; and finally, in *The Human Age,* an attempt to relate this action to the cosmic situation of mankind.

At the same time, and here the critic must be cautiously speculative, Lewis sought to come to terms with final things by an inspection and criticism of his long career as a highly intelligent, strong-willed Enemy. Proud assertions of self, like the one seen in the passage from *Time and Western Man* that is quoted at the beginning of this chapter, are not allowed to stand as the exclusive last word, though neither are they sentimentally rejected and apologized for by an old campaigner gone soft. But the strange, almost paradoxical, doubleness of response that had always characterized Lewis' obsessive dealings with matters of the self and the will persists: on the one hand, there is a condemnation of action and the self-willed "actor"—Vincent Penhale for example; on the other, a fascinated admiration for such energy and a recognition at least implicitly, that he, Lewis, possessed it himself. These impulses, among others, animate the writer's last books and attempt to clarify themselves.

I   Rotting Hill

Before his fiction and criticism of the 1950's began to appear, Lewis published *Rude Assignment,* a last enormous effort to explain, justify, qualify, and assert once more various positions he had taken—or had been accused by others of taking. An invaluable document about his past as revealed in the books he wrote, it is perhaps not to be read through or appreciated as an entity so much as to be consulted for the backgrounds and outlines of controversies and misunderstandings. Ideally, *Rude Assignment* was to clear the air and reveal what a considerable writer (and, incidentally, splendid chap) was Mr. Wyndham Lewis. There is no indication that the book accomplished this objective, but with the publication of *Rotting Hill* in the following year Lewis entered a period when, for the first time since the late 1920's, he was accorded some kind of recognition, however embarrassed or grudging it often sounded. But the relative attention he enjoyed did not affect the character of his books—as contrasted with the way a much greater public recognition encouraged Faulkner's self-congratulatory rhetoric during the same period. Mr. Rose is undeniably right when he suggests that the evidence of the letters shows the Enemy to have mellowed, yet no softening of fiber is to be found in the novels and short stories that are explicitly preoccupied with the human condition in an epoch of more bad times than were dreamt of in the 1930's.

Generalizing about the concerns of this fiction must take account of the fact that it varies greatly within itself as to quality: *Rotting Hill,* and even more so *The Red Priest,* are vastly inferior to *Self Condemned* and *The Human Age;* still, the books are united in that none of them displays technique as an object for admiration. It is instructive to compare the austerely highbrow opening of *Tarr* ("Paris hints of sacrifice. But here we deal with that large dusty facet known to indulgent and congruous kind:") with these sentences from the Foreword to *Rotting Hill:* "If I write about a hill that is rotting, it is because I deplore rot. For the decay of which I write is not romantic decay. . . . If we exist, shabby, ill-fed, loaded with debt (taxed more than any men at any time have ever been), let us recognize that the sole explanation of this is our collective stupidity. . . . The most *recent* wars have entirely altered our lives, that is all we can say." This alteration seems to be of such magnitude as to make stylistic inventiveness inappropriate, an anachronistic survival in the age of socialism and the welfare state; and certainly it is true that the stories in this book exhibit a lessened vitality consonant with the low-grade pain that throbs through most of them.

The book's title was suggested, Lewis tells us coyly in a footnote, by "a friend in Washington" who had gleefully penetrated to what truly underlay his Notting Hill address. The friend, residing in Washington in a rather special sense, was Ezra Pound; the "rot" had in fact invaded Lewis' apartment; and in the story of that title he imagines a snarling carpenter addressing him with axe in hand: "You can keep your plaster and your rotten wood, Mr. Lewis! *You* are the dry rot I'm after" (99). Lewis, who is on stage through most of the volume, finds himself harried by plumbers and carpenters, cultivated by a socialist clergyman who wants to buy one of his pictures ("The Bishop's Fool"), and plagued by a devotee of spontaneous child art ("My Disciple") or by an up-to-date undergraduate with strong leftist opinions ("My Fellow-

Traveler to Oxford"). Clearly it is difficult to generate much dramatic excitement when the author, in *propria persona*, lounges about receiving visitors or dealing with workmen; so the best parts of these often too relaxed narratives are the conversations about England's postwar experiment and attempted recovery. Their thinness as art is evident in that they do not deepen upon rereading; this remark will not sound like carping when we add that *Rotting Hill* is the first of Lewis' fictions about which it could be made.

Although the stories contain a few bright moments of well-being, their prevailing atmosphere is one of failure. It is often assumed, mistakenly, that *Rotting Hill* is simply a document of Lewis' own contempt and hatred for socialist Britian; this reading can be arrived at only by disregarding much of what happens in the stories and by ignoring the biographical note that very obviously enters them. Lewis' letters reveal that he had staked a good deal on his knowledge, even his hope, that the postwar world would be a new era, though he knew also that to be reborn into it might well be a grueling process, especially as old age came on. In a letter to Sturge Moore, previously quoted, the placid world of Hampstead domesticity was looked back on, but not to the obscuring of future necessities: "Whereas the very scale and intensity of the misery that will threaten every nation afterwards will assure heroic measures of public control, which automatically should end the selfish chaos into which our western society had drifted—I hope I am not too sanguine" (*L*, 292). Whether or not Lewis was sanguine, the stories in *Rotting Hill* testify that even war and exile could not turn the professional satirist into a revolutionary enthusiast. What they did instead was take most of the joy out of the satire, and replace it with a combination of annoyance and self-reproach; it is as if the carpenter had really said to Mr. Lewis that "*You* are the dry rot I'm after."

In only one story, "Time the Tiger," does Lewis manage to objectify his conflicting responses to the new society. It is in the heart of the story's hero, Mark Robins, that the low-grade pain is concentrated; and his heart is in tune with the London morning: "The sky was a constipated mass, yellowed by the fog, suspending over a city awaiting the Deluge" (163). The pain finds ample correlation in the most unpromising of materials for the encouragement of anything but low-grade action: shirts with too small buttonholes, too short shoelaces, vulgarly colored postwar tweeds, uncuttable bread, a tea made by combining "alleged Darjeeling" with "pseudo Ceylon," and, for breakfast, something called Strawberry Jam "recognized by housewives as mainly pectin / or carrot pulp, given appropriate colour of course and flavor to match" (169).

Mark's best friend, Charles Dyat, has decided not to cooperate with the new austerity but to make use of whatever bribes and other shady devices can improve creature comforts. To Charles' cynicism, Mark responds with an earnest defense of the Labour government, and eventually makes the point that he is not a convert to socialism but rather has been reborn a socialist since the world in which he and Charles grew up no longer exists. The seeing of an Existententialist film *Time the Tiger* is the occasion for an extension of the argument about immediate effects and harassments into the philosophic; it is Mark's tendency to replace the image of time as devourer with a less melodramatic one—that of time as a firework fizzling away. And indeed, at dinner with Charles' sister Ida, who is a romantic image of timelessness for Mark, things fizzle away: the Dyats insult Bevan and the socialists; Mark is shocked and annoyed; the dinner and the relationship fall to pieces.

Nothing would have been easier, especially considering what Lewis' fiction has made of previous men of commitment, to expose Mark's naïveté and have him learn something about the incommensurability of politics and the individual. But such an easy score is no longer open to Lewis—at least in this story. The hero's depression is a product of trying to hold the idea of a socialist experiment in his mind while he spoons out strawberry pectin or whatever it may be; as such, the repression cannot be relieved by instant fictional solutions. Or to use another image, the rot is there; and no reason presents itself for its not remaining there in the foreseeable future.

Rotting Hill is the greyest and least artistic of Lewis' fictions because it virtually admits that the imagination is powerless and irrelevant in the new world to which men have been reborn. Yet, and this is the particular fascination and difficulty in dealing with such a work, this collection of stories is in many ways a more admirable and valuable book to have appeared in 1951 than the productions of writers who made the transition from an old world

to a new one with effortless smoothness.[2] The limitations of most
of these stories are obvious enough; their virtue as a collection
consists in the way they unfailingly place us in a material world—
England as a recuperating patient who may be doctored to death
by well-meaning socialist physicians.

More tentatively, the book is also Lewis' most candid and dis-
pirited questioning of the efficacy of imaginative style in such a
world. If the artist is really on the way out, then perhaps this most
important of fizzles should be registered by at least one writer.
There is a fanciful ending to the final story in the book titled "The
Rot-Camp," where the "I," Wyndham Lewis, encounters in a suit-
ably fantastic way first Roy Campbell and his retinue of bull-
baiting aficionados, then Augustus John out hunting once more
for gypsies, and finally Britannia herself looking shriveled and
wasted, begging for alms. The author responds by dropping a
lucky three-penny bit into her mug—which appears to contain a
phony dollar bill: "In a cracked wheeze she sang 'Land of Hope
and Glory.' I must confess that this last apparition, and its vulgar
little song, rather depressed me" (307). That Lewis then proceeded to disregard his own prediction of the extinction of art and
to transform his depression into something else is the really marvelous story of the novels that follow *Rotting Hill.*

II   The Writer and the Absolute

Depression, however, is still the major note of Lewis' final venture in political and literary analysis, *The Writer and the Absolute*, which appeared in the following year. In it he makes his last
and perhaps most compelling plea for the novelist's freedom: his
necessary detachment from political partisanship at least insofar
as he is a novelist. For in that role he is concerned only with the
truth—*"what is"*; all else is merely the fictive, and may be equated
with the rapidly spreading dry rot recently encountered in another context. In a new and revealing gesture Lewis aligns the
novelist with the contemporary "scientific" historian as a teller of
"God's truth"; if the truth of a great novelist is more personal
than that of the good contemporary historian, it shares the same
disinterested motive—"a meticulous fidelity to life is of its es-
sence" (15).

This defense of the individual intelligence as an instrument of
truth does not open the door to idiosyncratic doing-as-one-likes.

As far back as *The Art of Being Ruled* Lewis had been concerned with the misleading and unsatisfactory character of such "freedom"; that of the great novelist, by contrast, consists in his necessity to render life with fidelity; and such rendering is possible because of the individual novelist or historian's "remarkable capacity for non-identity, or abstraction" (20). A vocabulary featuring terms like these suggests at first glance that Lewis might have been having second thoughts about his wholesale rejection of Eliot's "impersonal" theory of poetry; or perhaps he was working toward some version of Keatsian negative capability as distinctive of the true artist's "non-identity."

Looked at again though, it can be seen that the concern is not primarily directed at the achieved impersonality of the work of art, nor at the novelist's ability to imagine various and conflicting attitudes without resolving them into a single truth—although neither of these qualities is irrelevant to his work. If the freedom is not ideally the freedom to do as one likes, there is still no suggestion, as with Eliot's theory, that an individual talent needs to curb and tame its lawlessness or heresy by submission to tradition. Instead, the effort, an immense one which the novelist must make, is to elude the embrace of the political absolute that would seduce and turn him into a party man.

In this volume the party men, for all their internal differences, are the Existentialists, particularly Sartre, who is made the hero of the book since he figures as one of the *least* free men Lewis knows about. The analysis of Sartre, Camus, and Malraux takes up much of the volume; it follows traditional Lewis lines in that Existentialist heroics are considered as a contemporary (and highly successful) updating of the cult of will and action explored in *Tarr*, in *Time and Western Man,* and in the novels of the 1930's. Although Lewis makes it clear that he is not writing literary criticism, the brilliance of remarks made almost in passing sets up a base on which a full criticism of the particular writer could be mounted.

For example, we have a description of Sartre's *L'Âge de Raison* as in part "a muddled and intellectually rather squalid self-reproachful comedy" (110); or of Camus' *L'Étranger* as "an admirably written (though not otherwise I am afraid very admirable" novel (87); or, best of all, a reference to Malraux's "homosexual homicidal romantics," or to the author himself whose life has been all action "the penalty of which—from the writer's standpoint—is that the vitality of his books is only borrowed from his life, and less dense than it otherwise would be" (88). And, although compared to *Men Without Art*, *The Writer and the Absolute* exhibits less of Lewis' destructive wit, it flashes out a times with undiminished point—in reference, say, to the romantic homicides in Malraux's novels:

A lot of dialectic accompanies this ecstatic taking of life in Malraux's stories, however. The second line of the first page of *La Condition Humaine* contains the word "angoisse". . . . . This is one of the words some people get tired of reading in his books; it occurs very often. Tchen is discovered about to murder a man lying inside a mosquito net. I speak of this event most humbly as a mere *puceau:* but would a tough Chinese have quite so many sensations (of a European kind) while going about this little bit of revolutionary business? Would he experience "une atmosphere de folie," etc.?

(93–94)

What makes the treatment of these Continental writers more than ill-natured sniping is Lewis' admiration for the vitality of their books and their refusal to pretend they do not live in the twentieth century. In contrast, there was little going on in the English novel after the war that could have comparably brought out Lewis' most fruitful critical ambivalence: admiration for the writer's surface, his style; distaste for the assumptions or "worldview" behind that style (as in the case of Joyce, Pound, Hemingway, Eliot.)

The one English novelist who is permitted entry into this company of writers engaged with the political absolute is George Orwell. Lewis requested that a copy of *The Vulgar Streak* be sent to Orwell in 1941; however, after Orwell made an ill-advised crack in *Partisan Review* about Lewis' rumored conversion to communism(!), feelings were somewhat less warm; Orwell is referred to in the *Letters* as "Borewell" and is attacked in *Rude Assignment*. But mutual abuse shouldn't be allowed to obscure their literary relationship. Orwell's inclusion in the book under discussion is made not on the grounds, it is argued, that he is the only English writer worthy of attention since the war, but that he is an important example of the political writer who was locked in a struggle with the Absolute from which he almost broke free on his deathbed.

Lewis' treatment of Orwell contains certain distortions; if he is right to upgrade the disenchanted political sanity of *Animal Farm* and *1984* in contrast to the lately overrated prewar novels, he overlooks qualities in *The Road to Wigan Pier,* and particularly in *Homage to Catalonia,* which admirably reveal that very sanity. It should be emphasized, in other words, that Orwell had a respectable number of moments of freedom even before he wrote the final novels. Still, the analysis as a whole is the best thing on Orwell that exists. Lewis' depiction of him as a "romantic Scot" with a "dour pigheaded type of New-Statesmanlike social conscience," combined with a strong streak of snobbery and an obsession with bad smells, is psychologically acute and wholly relevant to Orwell's struggle for freedom. The justice of sending him *The Vulgar Streak* becomes apparent since Orwell, a kind of Vincent Penhale in reverse, has plunged into the life of action and has played the actor in a series of successively down-and-out social roles. More importantly, Orwell himself had already given terse expression to the warning that lies behind *The Writer and the Absolute:* "On the whole the literary history of the 'thirties' seems to justify the opinion that a writer does well to keep out of politics. For any writer who accepts or partially accepts the discipline of a political party is sooner or later faced with the alternative: toe the line, or shut up. . . ."[3]

It is more than likely that the emphasis Lewis gives to Orwell's eventual breakthrough to political realism is not simply a disinterested observation on another writer but his way of suggesting by implication that a similar transcendence took place in his own career. We have seen his own admission in letters written during World War II that he had thought too little of the "genre humain." His "anti-war" campaign of the 1930's involved, whether or not he ever fully recognized it, a cultivated disregard of excesses of the Right, while he roundly abused those of the Left. This defection from the true *clerc's* detachment was a capitulation to the Absolute and a mark of Lewis' own lack of freedom—although in *The Revenge for Love* he created a tragic action beyond politics, even if the satirical parts of the book were heavily directed at the Left.

Generally, in the two decades between the wars, the repeated note is that politics should fade away and let the artist get on with his business. Lewis, I think, came to feel that this attitude was less detachment than wishful thinking. Or, put another way, the contention makes sense as long as the artist's business is satirizing Apes of God or pseudo-humanity in general. In 1952, however, with another war done and with parties at Lord Osmund's no longer a central image for England, it may have been doubted whether the artist—and particularly the novelist—would ever be let alone again. In the face of political threats to freedom of a magnitude undreamt of in the 1930's, Lewis made his appeal, for the first time, to the community of writers. The virtues he pled for were old-fashioned ones that men of that community like E. M. Forster or Orwell himself had been plugging for: tolerance and good sense; keeping free the channels of creativity. Lewis does not ask the writer to turn his back on politics; indeed, he had just written that it was impossible for a work to contain less politics than *Rotting Hill* did. But the novelist's highest allegiances must be non-political, and to recognize them is to take the first step toward being able to live with politics itself.

Although tolerance and good sense are now ideal, recommended virtues, when we look at the postwar books discussed above, to which should be added the brief *Demon of Progress in the Arts* (1954), we breathe an air of overall depression to an extent unencountered before in Lewis' work. The *Demon* has a rather disturbing last paragraph which concludes morosely that its subject—the alarming outlook for the fine arts—seems finally trivial, since it is "infected with the triviality of everything else." There is also in that paragraph a reference to bodily deterioration and a particularly pointed mention of "our wonderful shining eyes" that Nature is making duller and more myopic each year. The point is not, of course, that anything is "explained" by reminders that Lewis' vision was hazy by 1951 and totally gone by 1953. What most persists and nags is not the note of physical deprivation but the knowledge, expressed with both wit and bitterness in *Rude Assignment,* that his audience was painfully limited and that, even with the few recognitions received during the 1950's, it would take a more sanguine view of the world than the one he habitually held to expect a radical upturn in his influence.

Still, it is misleading to claim that the final books are preoccupied with the inevitable failure and defeat of self, and then proceed to reduce them to purely sentimental revelations of personal disquiet. The reduction needn't occur since the books in their various ways are thick with "what is"—with the truth of fact, of analysis, and of novelistic invention. *Rotting Hill* would be merely a testy personal gripe if it were not crammed with the often fascinating stuff of life in postwar London. And although *Rude Assignment, The Writer and the Absolute,* and *The Demon of Progress in the Arts* are very much about the failure of Wyndham Lewis to become a successful painter, a best-selling novelist, and a generally respected sage, they are not lyrical cries of puzzled despair but grimly ironic analyses of how this phenomenon took (or rather didn't take) shape. In this substantiation, personal eclipse or failure becomes representative of the possible fate of a kind of artist in the modern world. And in these terms we can approach the two major works of fiction of his final years: *Self Condemned* and *The Human Age,* books whose assault on the reader is no less than total. They are filled with the combined truths of fact, analysis, and invention; whatever their virtues and limitations as novels there are no other works in modern literature like them.

III   Self Condemned

As early as 1947 in a letter to a publisher, Lewis spoke of what was eventually to become *Self Condemned:*

. . . The novel I am proposing to write is not a satire—like "The Apes of God." It will be a straight novel, a normal narrative, as much as "Tarr" for instance: or—oh, Mr. Morgan's "Fountain." As now planned it will be dominated by the "everything or nothing" principle. This means a character who is what today colloquially is known as a perfectionist. Woman has been called "the eternal enemy of the absolute": so our perfectionist must encounter immediate difficulties when he comes in contact with women.

No such man as this, I should add, is known to me, so no one could say (as in the case of Meredith's "Egoist" for instance) that I had founded the character on him. In any case, the character is not displeasing.

(L, 410)

The mild defense of his hero's character should be balanced with a later remark, made after the book was written, to an admirer who thought the hero reminded her of her husband. Lewis said he hoped that she was mistaken and advised her that to be like his hero was "very dangerous."

148

WYNDHAM LEWIS

This dwelling on character is understandable if we examine the kind of "straight novel" or "normal narrative" the book in fact turned out to be. The colorless adjectives "straight" and "normal" suggest that verbal effects appropriate to *The Apes of God* will, of course, be absent; so too the arty complication of that earlier "straight novel" *Tarr;* and even the finely orchestrated stylistic components of *The Revenge for Love*. With respect to Lewis' previous novels, *Self Condemned* most resembles *The Vulgar Streak* in its gravely sardonic unity of tone; but the differences are much more significant. The story of Vincent Penhale's collapse is put together with a strongly economical selectivity and with a highlighting of detail in which certain themes are firmly established; there is a metaphorical design to the novel that suggests its affiliations with more abstract forms—the fairy tale or the comic fable. *Self Condemned* has its own affinities with the fable, and the metaphorical meanings of certain objects and events are clearly brought out; but an insistent, even obsessive, *literalness* is the real source of its authority. Probably never before in a Lewis novel has a protagonist been so surrounded and expressed by things in all their literal being, especially when the book concentrates on the furniture of life in a Canadian hotel.

Matters of plot need detain us in only a summary way: René Harding on the eve of World War II quits his professorship of history at an English university because he no longer believes in what he is teaching, bids good-bye to his mother, his three married sisters, and his intellectual disciple "Rotter" Parkinson, and sails for Canada with his wife Hester. These events occupy the first third of the novel titled "The Resignation." Section Two which describes, often with affecting intensity, the Hardings' life in their twenty-five-feet-by-twelve room at the Hotel Blundell, Momaco (Toronto), is simply and most strikingly titled "The Room." Their seclusion ends when the hotel burns down, and the final section of the book—"After the Fire"—interweaves René's gradual capitulation to the academic life he had rejected, with Hester's growing unhappiness and disaffection, culminating in her suicide. After René makes the necessary adjustments, he accepts a job in an American university, and the book ends.

Hugh Kenner has picturesquely termed *Self Condemned* "not a well-made novel but a slow and terrible wind,"[4] yet it should be admitted, without disrespect to Lewis' achievement, that it is also a windy book, rambling and at times almost intolerably discursive, particularly in the Canadian sections. In consulting the manuscript material for the novel, Mr. Rose found that Lewis had conceived an alternative conclusion to the book in which René would return to Europe to struggle with postwar adversities. While Rose argues sensibly that Lewis made the right choice in rejecting this alternative,[5] its presence in the novelist's mind does not necessarily make the working-out of the actual book any firmer; and there are instances of arbitrary and summary treatment of characters whom the author has not decided just how seriously to take.

More importantly, with regard to René himself, Lewis manifests an ambivalence of feeling that makes it dangerous to accept too quickly the terms offered by the closing paragraphs of the novel: a hero who confronts the gods and is struck down twice, the second time with crippling consequences. We have Lewis' word that it is "very dangerous" to be like René; it is dangerous surely to tempt the gods, but perhaps dangerous also for an enthusiastic reader to adopt such inflammatory and heroic language. Because of the book's strongly autobiographical cast and its memorable pictures of the room, the fire, and Hester's death, it can be admired for its portraits of bleakness and deprivation in a way Lewis' other books could scarcely be. As we shall see later, part of this admiration is shared by the author himself in his more sympathetic and unguarded moments.

Although the early section of *Self Condemned* moves along smoothly enough, it has no striking effects. The harshness of the perfectionist hero is established at the same time that his vulnerability to family sentiment is insisted upon. This sentiment does not extend to his wife Hester, whose feelings about leaving England are either pointedly ignored by René or overcome by his sexual ardors. On the other hand, he takes leave of his sister Helen in a moment of pathos:

He put his arm around her waist, and tears came into his eyes. "We must part, Sister. I am afraid we shall not meet again. Everything is over with me, you know, I feel." He put his head down to her shoulder, and she could feel him shake . . .

"René,"—she spoke to him softly—"why are you like this?"

René looked up, intelligence appearing to return. "Sadness, you

know, at parting," he said drily. "At leaving everything, at going away
into a wilderness among so very solid a mass of strangers. And never
to come back. Never to come back."

(137)

There is little to say about this passage, typical of many in the
novel, except that it describes a common, strong emotion in words
no less common. Such moments leave us agitated rather than contemplative as we share the hero's unease. Lewis seems willing that
it should be so; that is, there is little pressure of form exerted on
these moments to shape them into essentially literary experience
—as was always the case in his previous novels. This observation
points again to the literalness of *Self Condemned,* its willingness
—extraordinary, considering Lewis' former practices—to present
life with a minimal emphasis on the presentation. And the life
presented, disturbs.

The most disturbing creation in the novel is the room in which
the Hardings spend their early Canadian years. In the following
sample from the opening pages of Section Two, the literal transforms itself into the fantastic as we read:

The Room, in the Hotel Blundell, was twenty-five feet by twelve
about. It was no cell. It was lit by six windows: three composed a
bay, in which well-lit area they spent most of their time— . . .
They never left the room, these two people, except to shop at the
corner of the block. They were as isolated as are the men of the police-
posts on Coronation Gulf or Baffin Bay. They were surrounded by a
coldness as great as that of the ice-pack; but this was a human pack
upon the edge of which they lived . . .
. . . They must vegetate, violent and morose—sometimes blissfully
drunken, sometimes with no money for drink—within these four walls,
in the identical daily scene—from breakfast until the time came to
tear down the Murphy bed, to pant and sweat in the night tempera-
ture kicked up by the radiators—until the war's end or the world's end
was it? Until they had died or become different people and the world
that they had left had changed its identity too, or died as they had
died . . .

(168–71)

This prose develops its own droning intensity because, in part, of
the awkward (in other places, just careless) repetitions and insist-
ences. Yet the literal catalogue of what "they" did and suffered

does not seem merely a dutiful filling-in of a typical day with the Hardings in Momaco; instead, after the space of a few descriptive paragraphs, "they" have already become remote and unearthly. The medium in its glazed intensity of presentation bids fair to transform them into creatures of romantic fable—and the list of strange wonders at the Hotel Blundell is indeed endless. The alternative poised so off-handedly after the dash—"until the war's end or the world's end was it?"—suggests that, on the heroic moral plane which René has chosen, any human act may be transformed into a pure and inhuman act. The perfectionist can stop at no less.

The repetitive insistence of the book's prose and the asperity of its hero recall no writer so much as D. H. Lawrence, whom Lewis had mocked and castigated for his romantic primitivism. We can imagine that, if Lewis were challenged about the style of *Self Condemned* and charges pressed of windiness, lack of variety, saying the same thing three different ways—along with other matters of ungainly transitions and character introductions—he might well have replied with a defense similar to Lawrence's in the preface to *Women in Love*: "The only answer is that it is natural to the author." The harsh unhappiness and heroic pretensions of René Harding are also related to such qualities in the hero of *Women in Love*—Rupert Birkin—in actual display though not in theoretical motivation. The hero of each novel is subjected to varieties of criticism from other characters: Birkin, largely and effectively by Ursula; René, initially by his mother, whose question "You are not by any chance a *fool*, my son?" reverberates through the book; and, finally, by the words and then by the suicide of his wife Hester.

A more complicated and important affinity between the books lies in the author's neglect of "point of view." It is impossible with Lewis-René, as with Lawrence-Birkin, to make clear distinctions between the writer's sentiments and those of the hero. Much of the time they are shared, but there are other moments when we guess they are not (the impulse in this case is critical and satirical) or when we are uncertain. This uncertainty points up the crucial difficulty in reading Lewis' and Lawrence's novels; in *Self Condemned* and in *Women in Love* the hero is used by his creator to articulate and try out certain ideas about which the creator himself has not made up his mind. The resulting ambience—Leavis

would call it "exploratory-creative"—is impressive evidence in
Lewis' case that at the age of seventy-two his imagination was
more open to experience, in its common, moral, human aspects,
than had been the case thirty and forty years earlier. In this sense
Self Condemned is a more truly experimental book than either
Childermass or *The Apes of God*.

There are moments, it must be admitted, when the narrative
simply does not deserve the honorific bestowal of "exploratory-
creative." Neglect of point of view is at times merely narrative
slipperiness, a traditional resource of the English novelist. Thackeray for one was a past master at it; it has its own value and is
marked as a flaw only by the stricter disciples of Jamesian-
Conradian "telling." On the other hand, there is a relative feature,
common to both Lewis' and Lawrence's novels, that is harder to
accept or excuse: the narrator's willingness momentarily to set his
tale at naught by moving off into excursions and sermons. There
are blatant examples of this in *St. Mawr* and in *Women in Love*;
in *Self Condemned*, similarly, Lewis' style sometimes goes wildly
out of gear, and he begins to talk to himself.

For example, speaking of gross mismanagement at the Hotel
Blundell, he writes: "It was in no way more cock-eyed than the
city, however. I doubt if it was more ramshackle than any State. It
was madly ill-run. But are not all States ill-run? Are not most cities
glaringly mismanaged? Of course . . . For honestly you must
grant me this . . ." (190–91). Who must grant "this" to whom?
Novelist, hero, tale, and reader have disappeared alike into a
great stew of talk and opinion where anybody can say anything
about everything. It is not necessary to convict ourselves of arid
preferences for "well-made novels" if we wish for more artistry at
work. So too with the novel's prevailing uncertainty about tense,
manifested by a wandering into and out of the present; it is as if
Lewis, intent on setting down as many as possible of his experiences in wartime Toronto, could not fully transform them into the
imagined world of a novel, sufficient unto itself.

Yet out of these narrative vices great virtues unexpectedly
spring. It is difficult to lament the failure to transform experience
sufficiently when some of the most engaging parts of the "Room"
section are bits of clearly autobiographical memories and experiences in the recitation of which René Harding is forgotten, and
we hear only the accents of Wyndham Lewis, expatriate. After a

fine evocation of the hateful vacuum of a wartime Sunday, with its blaring radio proclaiming "a day of verbal blood-letting, of exhortations to homicides and quivering organpipes," the marvelous occurs: "But about seven o'clock Eastern war-time Jack Benny brings far more than comic-relief. He brings a great gust of reality and heaven-sent respite from Godliness—and from verbal thunder of bulletins telling of battles that probably were never fought (or not that way). A salvo of wisecracks dispels the fog. We are back on the earth again with Jack and Rochester, among things that matter to men, and things that are good for human consumption" (183).

Lewis returns to the same theme later on, saluting the other comedians with one particularly charming sentence: "They did not turn up their noses, either at Fibber Magee and his outfit: and they both felt the keenest displeasure if anything caused them to miss Gracie Allen . . ." (246). The truth and passion of these tributes is self-evident; and, of course, never was "point of view" more irrelevant. Any conflicting feelings about the novel's loose disregard for certain technical matters should be balanced by admitting that, as is the case with *Women in Love,* there are few modern books that provoke such a conflict.

A more serious matter for examination is the convincingness of Lewis' hero, particularly with regard to the validity of his motives for exile. This problem involves the autobiographical nature of the book, for speculation about Lewis' interest in creating a "perfectionist" hero is essential to sound out the resonance of the author's career in this late work. Although there is a great deal of talk about history throughout the novel, including a full text of "Rotter" Parkinson's long review of the hero's last book, we can fairly summarize René's slant by quoting the narrator's account of it. Like a good Cartesian, René is preoccupied with the miraculous phenomenon of consciousness: "No one could imagine why man had abstracted himself and acquired the sanity of consciousness; why he had gone sane in the midst of a madhouse of functional character.—And History: with that, René's central tragedy was reached. History, such as is worth recording, is about the passion of men to stop sane. Most History so-called is the bloody catalogue of their backslidings" (212). The historian should be talking about ideas, arts, inventions; but he preoccupies himself with wars, intrigues, and the "heros" of these enterprises. Finding himself in a false position, and unwilling to practice hypocrisy, René gives up his job, goes to Canada, and locks himself up in a hotel room where "the passion of men to stop sane" is not remarkably in evidence. In fact, the hotel is presented as an image of the world's chaos; in René's words, "It is an astonishingly violent place, but no more violent than is the world of which it is so perfect a microcosm" (231).

Without arguing that there is "really" another motive behind René's resignation, it is hard to accept it as the ruthlessly honest act he conceives it to be. Who are the powers or people that decree history must be taught in a certain way? They are surely not there in the life of the novel. Even if the reader is willing to convict himself of unheroic concerns in criticizing the resignation and flight, it is essential that he be able to imagine the logic of action on a higher heroic plane. But there is simply not enough information given to permit that possibility; the result is that René's act takes on a wilder and stranger aspect—that of absolute repudiation. In the case of Lewis' own exile, he was at pains to insist a number of times on its economic necessity. There seems little reason to doubt the seriousness of his financial straits and his assumption that the coming war would make England a bad place in which to recoup his losses. But, in writing the novel, he must have felt that his own reasons for leaving England were too inglorious to serve the perfectionist hero of his conception, as well as too sanely compromising with circumstances—however much events were to prove him wrong on the last count.

The tendency of the perfectionist hero toward absolute repudiation is dramatized in striking gestures and events, the way a more compromising leave-taking could not be. Mentioned previously were the agonies of parting, and, perhaps most strikingly, the vicious jettisoning of effects that René engages in. This jettisoning is felt most sharply as on shipboard he begins to read George Eliot's *Middlemarch*. Oppressed by its "sodden satire," its "lifeless realism," he decides that it is a part of history and thereupon hurls the "dull nonsense" overboard. Perhaps the gesture is fully shocking only if we believe that the man who is tired of *Middlemarch* is tired of Life, but it is revealing that Lewis chose to have his hero forcefully reject the most human of books. This action suggests that the perfectionist's inability to take in the imperfect world depicted by George Eliot is a measure of his own limitation. The inability is most pronounced in René's attitudes toward sexual matters. His conjugal pleasures are treated alternately as a venture into the absurd, a foolish and slightly humiliating weakness, and at most a disquieting and disgusting betrayal of his true self—what Lewis terms with some irony "the masterful analyst." Once again the protagonist's limitations are brought out by the novel, whatever mixed feelings Lewis himself entertained toward them. Although nothing that René's wife says or does strikes us as contemptible or foolish, she is presented in the early part of the novel as a large, vacant-minded, cowlike figure of lubricity. The husbands of René's three sisters range from fools to knaves; finally, the homosexuals appear in Momaco and are provided their share of mockery and annoyed contempt. Imperfections of love, like those of society and history, are grist for the mill of the masterful analyst.

Clearly, the intellectual's rejection of so-called history involves other rejections of the human that cast René in a not wholly sympathetic light. There have, of course, been other masterful analysts in Lewis' fiction. The first and most engaging of them, Tarr, was punished comically for his asperity by being awarded two women when one had been too much. *Self Condemned*, forty years later, is more severe in the punishment it metes out. Hester's suicide, committed in the face of René's capitulation to Canada and a new, if second-rate, life, proves finally to be more than the analyst can master. His fate is to be "a glacial shell of a man" condemned to an American university—evidently a sufficiently horrible fate. It has been pointed out that the title of the book is a pun: René's self is condemned to this new "life," and René did the condemning. But the words reach out to broader implications if we admit that the most masterful of all analysts (so he always felt!) was Lewis himself; and that, as he punished comically an earlier intransigent—the prewar bohemian Tarr—he now punishes with a grim thoroughness his avatar in the gritty 1940's and 1950's, René Harding.

John Holloway in a discussion of Shakespearean tragedy has found that its attention is "fixed upon the career and ordeal of a protagonist who makes . . . the great refusal; who progressively cuts himself off from the normal fabric of human society and interdependence. . . . Yet also, as the play proceeds, this great repudiator of the common fabric of life is repudiated by what he repudiates; and after a protracted ordeal of suffering which displays the full measure of what it is he has chosen as a way of life, meets a death which is frequently accepted as appropriate for him both by himself, and by those in the play who are most on his side." [6] Whether or not René's "death" is appropriate, it is surely relevant to think of *Self Condemned* as a tragic novel. The book is not, as the jacket spritely tells us, about the "heroism of the unorthodox" which is vindicated as "in a new country his [René's] revolutionary theories find acceptance," but about what it costs a man and those around him when what Holloway calls "the great refusal" is made—when the heroic moral plane of action is chosen and the self rises to it. It is *this* self that Wyndham Lewis condemns through the novel, condemning along with it—though not repenting or attempting to take it back—his own infallible rectitude as individual and enemy. Like Shakespearean tragedy, the novel does not say "That is wrong, you know" but "That is what happens, you see;" and thereby the condemnation of self becomes dignified rather than abject.

IV   The Human Age

Of a conversation held with Lewis in 1956, Hugh Kenner reports that he disclaimed interest in his earlier books and hoped that he would be remembered for *The Human Age*.[7] Like Tolstoy, Lewis evidently felt that his late work embodied a spiritual and moral pattern which transcended purely esthetic considerations and made his earlier work of limited relevance. *The Human Age* not only judges the self, but condemns it by the very inclusiveness of the world that self imagines. It deserves to be read as Wyndham Lewis' last word on that subject; yet it is the opposite of a sacred book for the initiate or cultist. It means instead, quiet patently, to delight (or terrify) and instruct. Its ideal audience is the common reader who, by nature, must be engaged with the subject since it is of ultimate concern to him.

Circumstances of the book's publication are more important than usual and can be stated briefly. It was announced as Lewis' long awaited continuation of *The Childermass*—published almost thirty years previously—and as forming Parts Two and Three, *Monstre Gai* and *Malign Fiesta*, of a projected four-part epic. The fourth and concluding part was only projected; Lewis died in March, 1957, and left but a synopsis and a manuscript version of the opening scene. Parts Two and Three, referred to here as *The Human Age,* present some justification for arguing that they represent the epic in its significant entirety. As was suggested previously, they have only the flimsiest, most abstract relationship with the earlier *Childermass.* The characters, James Pullman, Satters, and the Bailiff turn up again, now inside the Magnetic City; but they are no longer presented to us in the pretentious verbiage of "experimental" writing. And, although *The Childermass* was republished in 1956, it was altered only very slightly and in no sense does it belong stylistically or morally with its continuation. The projected fourth part, *The Trial of Man,* must be regarded with as much uncertainty as the plays Keats was about to write. Ill as he was, Lewis found time to write and publish a final novel, *The Red Priest,* and virtually to complete another—*Twentieth Century Palette*— instead of executing the more difficult and demanding finale of Pullman's adventures. Without making necessity the mother of too much invention, there is a case for claiming that *The Human Age* should end where it does, with Pullman carried away into the Divine element, whatever outcome the uplifting— call it "rescue" or "capture"—was to have.

The spiritual and moral pattern already mentioned can easily be discerned from the baldest narrative summary. In *Monstre Gai* Pullman and Satters gain entrance to the Magnetic City—Third City, it is now called—to find that it is not Heaven but a sort of purgatory. Ruled by a beautiful if ineffectual angel called the Padishah, the place contains both enervating leisure and fierce political contention. When this contention reaches a pitch during Pullman's stay there, he resolves to locate the point of maximum power and to throw his hand in with it, regardless of any private qualms. That point, so it appears, is located not in the Padishah but in the Gay Monster himself—the cynical clubmanesque Bailiff. Pullman duly joins the Bailiff's party, although, as predicted, some stifling of private conscience is necessary; late in the book in a gigantic four-way public argument among the Bailiff, Hyperides (the Lewisian advocate of *Childermass,* now a simple Fascist), a Communist, and a Catholic priest, the cleric's voice makes itself felt as Pullman turns sadly away: " . . . for he knew that that was the only voice, in this place of oratory, to which he had any right to respond, to which he would listen with more than a worldly—an all-too-worldly—tolerence" (253). The strength of

Pullman's response comes as a surprise since there has been little preparation for such an awareness. But the note recurs and grows in intensity: eventually matters in Third City worsen as inner unrest combines with a devilish attack from outside; Pullman and Satters fly with the Bailiff to Hell—a city called "Matapolis"—and the events of *Malign Fiesta* commence.

In Matapolis, the Baliff becomes a much less resplendent or promising figure when Pullman locates the point of maximum power in the Devil himself—the Lord Sammael, ruler of Dis and governor of the fallen Angels who live in Angeltown. Like any good Lewis devil, Sammael is a revolutionary. Bored with Hell as it now is, he plans to humanize the fallen angels and thus reduce to meaninglessness the opposition between Heaven and Hell. With Pullman's valuable assistance, a sort of Princeton Institute for Advanced Studies is set up in Angeltown where the humanizing can go on among first-rate fallen-angel specimens. But Pullman has been receiving signs from Heaven that his time is at hand; the book ends with forcible demonstration of this as, in an ocean of light, two White Angels burst into his room; and he imagines a voice saying that Mr. Pullman is being carried away by two of God's servants.

Pullman is spiritually ready for the visitation. He now entertains quite other thoughts than the earlier all-too-human ones about locating the point of maximum power: "God *values* man: that is the important thing to remember. It is this valuing that is so extraordinary. There are men who only value *power*. This is absurd, because power destroys value. Value can only exist with multiplicity. . . . I, Pullman, am acting in a valueless vacuum called Sammael" (528). As his involvement with Sammael becomes complete, so does his guilt at assisting with the "annihilation of the Divine" (511). The momentous debate between the Human and the Divine, the projected subject of *The Trial of Man*, was to make clear Pullman's final allegiance and to resolve his fate. From the evidence of the letter to Hugh Kenner, there is no doubt where Lewis and his hero stood: "he favours the Divine; I favour the Divine" (*L*, 652). The problem, of course, would have been to render this preference in a valid fictional action. As for the completed books, we can note that, if Pullman's spiritual progress in *The Human Age* lacks gradations—there is a rather sudden awakening in *Malign Fiesta* to the damning consequences of his actions—the main direction is, nevertheless, clear enough: from fear and uncertainty, to rationalized prudence and *realpolitik*, to a shuddering realization that it wasn't prudence at all and that the valuing of Man by the Divine is past reason and politics alike.

The interesting critical question which the book raises, especially for a reader of Lewis' other works, concerns the nature of our literary response to these large issues. Perhaps the main line of answer to his question was suggested by Mr. Eliot in his "Note on *Monstre Gai*" that ran in *Hudson Review* along with selections from the soon-to-be-published novel. Eliot not only committed himself to *suspecting* that Lewis was "the greatest prose master of style of my generation" (the poet admitted that, of course, he didn't keep up on fiction), but he also detected a "development in humanity" in the extension of Pullman's adventures, especially when compared with the earlier *Childermass*.[8] The development in humanity, Eliot would probably have agreed, was no sudden product of the 1950's, as *The Revenge for Love* and *The Vulgar Streak* attest. But, since Lewis is now trying to write finally about "All there is," a critic whose religious persuasions were positive and evident would see development in the placing of a hero, a human being, a writer, in the most inclusive cosmic sense imaginable. Eliot himself, without attempting to lay out the furniture of heaven and hell, had imagined such inclusiveness through the generalizing ambition of *Four Quartets*. Eliot then singles out "a moment suggestive of the high tragedy of *Self Condemned* (a book of almost unbearable spirtual agony)" that occurs when Pullman sees his life in Third City repeating the pattern of his earthly one. So *The Human Age* may be linked with *Self Condemned*, despite their dissimilarity of mode and execution. The development in humanity noted would be inclined toward the tragic: in René Harding's case, the tragedy is unmitigated; in Pullman's, with supernatural valuing and a contrite heart, it might well be mitigated.

Yet assimilating the books in this way is misleading if it leads us to expect the same kind of intensive moral and spiritual energy—an "agony" Eliot calls it—in each. *The Human Age*, particularly in the *Malign Fiesta* section concerning the punishment cells of Dis, presents human torments as only professional expertise can devise; but these are something other than the painfully rendered ones of the protagonist of *Self Condemned*. Indeed, the whole composition of *The Human Age* is as measured and calm as the demeanor of its cautious hero. James Pullman has none of René Harding's extremist pretensions, neither his theoretical absolutism about the nature of history nor his inclination toward action on the high moral plane. The prose medium in which he moves is appropriately much more conserving of itself and more certain of its direction than the alternately garrulous or depressed narrative of *Self Condemned*.

At crucial points in Pullman's developing awareness of his position, the world of action seems to vanish altogether; its place is taken by contemplative analysis. The impulse of the book is always toward discovery and new understanding rather than toward presenting the hero in the grip of dramatic immediacy. For example, after the debate in the piazza of the Third City among Father Ryan, the Communist, Hyperides, and the Bailiff, Pullman realizes that the role a man played on earth pursues him afterwards; and he characterizes his own role as "essentially diabolic":

. . . —more and more clearly he understood that the point had been reached at which he was called upon to take a final decision. Should he take the emotional road, or the one indicated by common sense. He realized that upon Earth he had decided in favour of common sense, or, to put it in a more complimentary way, the logical and the practical. He had known that there was such a thing as the Right and the Wrong; that there was no such thing for a man, as "Beyond good and evil." That was merely the self-advertising eccentricity of an intellectual. Christianity apart, these values of Good and of Bad dominated human life, at its deepest level. On Earth, life was usually lived at a superficial level. Fundamental values played very little part in the conduct of life; and that was the reason for the frightful dilemma in which he found himself; because he inherited a superficial habit of mind.

(263–64)

Despite this analysis, Pullman decides to cast his lot with common sense and the Bailiff; he is unwilling to give his "superficial" commitment to earthly intelligence, self-interest, and common sense.

But it is less important to follow the chain of reasoning, or to ask whether the four orators represent an adequate cross-section of philosophic systems, than to be clear about what our own situation is with regard to Pullman. Compared with the debates between René Harding and his wife, or within René's own mind, Pullman's intellectual construings seem not to spring from any individual complexity or psychology. The reader is correspondingly remote and detached from him; in fact, "he" is really little more than a name, a convenient zone within which perceptions about large matters can fall. So the ordinary interests of "story" are absent; "which alternative will he choose" does not seem like a useful or necessary question to ask; and we read on instead to complete our own knowledge of the world he is discovering.

It would be as wrong to claim that Pullman is uninteresting or unreal as it would be to call him a dramatically convincing sufferer of tragic or near-tragic experience. Lewis' generalized scheme is such that his hero, although a man of high intelligence, must also represent Reasonable Man who possesses decency and prudence; preserves as best he can a well-balanced delight in the pleasures of the senses and the mind's activity; is urbane, witty, and charming by turns; recognizes the vicissitude of experience; and adopts a fundamentally serious attitude toward the worth of living. So, although a writer and a satirist, Pullman is otherwise lacking in the distortions, the "humours," that make the intellectual difficult; and there is an attendant absence of certain local involvements with what he himself refers to as "the self-advertising eccentricity of an intellectual." We are left with Pullman as a superior human specimen who has committed no sensational evil on earth, but who is nonetheless forced gradually, by conscience and by circumstance, to turn on his earthly prudent self and to admit its irrelevance in a way that a more obvious sinner would not.

Hugh Kenner rightly invokes Milton and Swift as the dead masters that most evidently preside over *The Human Age;*[9] yet, compared with Milton's *Pardise Lost* and Swift's *Gulliver's Travels,* the intellectual interest of the book—political, social, theological—is slight. Lewis' other last novels, *Self Condemned* and even *The Red Priest,* possess much more intellectual substance; indeed, both of them, particularly the second, are awkwardly packed with content that might well have found its place in an independent essay. The paradox is that this intellectual substance is the wordly air which the man of ideas breathes; and James Pullman has literally moved into a new region, a quite different ambience. Lewis is unable to make use of traditional myths he had paid little attention to all his life, as a context for complex intellectual discussion; nor can he call new ones into being to provide such a context. The reception we give to Pullman's analysis of the power situation in Third City may be interested and respectful, but it is different from the dramatic sympathies engaged, say, by Satan in Hell or by Gulliver in Houyhnhnm land.

The Human Age is not to be understood or valued primarily as a dramatic confrontation among ideas or ideologies, nor for its creation and penetration of a complex individual mind; its affinities, loosely adapting a phrase of J. R. R. Tolkien's, are rather with creative fantasy.[10] It is perhaps easier to say, therefore, what the book is *not* than what it is. Creative fantasy in Lewis' hands is not a verbal matter in the sense that it was in *The Childermass;* at the same time, though what Pullman sees is the substance of the book, it is not a highly visual, spectacular work. Instead, this substance emerges through the plainest of plain styles that neither concentrates fussily on the "outsides" of things, nor attempts to go deep into a "dark within," but is wed to a fertility of invention that makes the inside-outside issue no longer an issue. Putting it more positively, it is the experience of discovery above all else that the novel makes important: discovery that is felt through surprise, bemusement, admiration, and horror. In this respect, Pullman's receptivity—his tentative openness to the new—is reminiscent of the traditional heroic virtues of epic and romance. The lack of a complexly engaging inner drama can then be seen as one of the exigencies of the peculiar literary form that Lewis contrived.

These related points may be drawn together by reference to a crucial moment in the book that occurs as Pullman watches the Lord Sammael throw a woman—a "female sinner"—to the Yahoo-like creatures inhabiting the mountains outside Matapolis. In response to her cries of *"Pitié,"* Sammael flings open the door of the moving car; and she is snatched out by the beasts:

There was her body, shoulder-high, for the fraction of a second, in the midst of the stinking pack—the sickening odour increasing in intensity. Just for that fractional speck of time, a dozen claws could be seen defiling her person. The most terrible scream Pullman had ever heard filled aurally that speck of time. The car gathered speed, the door was violently closed, and that was that. The silence was tremendous and Pullman was alone—more alone than he had ever been with anyone in his life—with the lord Sammael.

. . . Pullman was trembling: the suddenness of the dénouement, and the shocking momentary vision of ferocity had deeply shaken him. The woman's denunciation of Sammael immediately before the climax had affected him in a way he had to be very careful not to reveal. His sympathy for the woman grew and subterraneously developed; and when he *saw* (with unexpected suddenness) the unsurpassable horror of her punishment he started trembling as in response to horror, because of the violent conflict in his psyche. He was on the verge of an outburst. The woman, praying and crossing herself, was doing what he ought to have been doing.

(372)

The power of this scene is not dependent on any complication of meaning or signification, or on any grace of style. Aspects of it are named almost naïvely: a "most terrible" scream, an "unsurpassable" horror, a "tremendous" silence, and Pullman "more alone than he had ever been with anyone in his life." This language tries to name an experience of absolute proportions and therefore eschews subtleties appropriate to more mundane and complex matters. So too the narrator fails to "dramatize" in the Jamesian sense; he merely asserts quite tonelessly about Pullman that the vision "had deeply shaken him," or that "He was on the verge of an outburst," or refers to "the violent conflict in his psyche." In short, nothing distracts us from what Pullman sees; the immediate and consequent horror is simply there. At its best, *The Human Age* is likewise "simply there"; and Lewis seems to acquire confidence as he moves along, particularly in *Malign Fiesta,* that the mode of telling is right for his purposes.

In a final attempt to say what the purpose is, let us return to the passage quoted above and ask: what can be made of its moral weight if it is assumed that, like Pound, Lewis built his hells for other people? The assumption in 1955 was about twenty-five years out of date, for it fitted only the satirist who flagellated apes of God. A few pages after throwing the female sinner to the beasts, Sammael, though he disclaims any enjoyment in executing such tasks, admits that "On principle, I approve of punishing Man just for being Man" (377). Truly, the wheel has come full circle if we recall Lewis' insistence in *Men Without Art* that, since all men are imperfect, everyone should be ridiculed.

The point is that it would have been quite possible at one time for Wyndham Lewis to meet with the Lord Sammael on terms of fastidious asperity; thus the meaning of Pullman's central meditation in *Monstre Gai*, about how one's earthly role is continued after death, becomes enriched. In that meditation the fictional hero found angelic perfection to be every bit as boring as was human virtue to the writer who would satirize all men, regardless of their moral character and aspirations. In other words, Pullman's role, like that of the earlier Lewis, was essentially diabolic; the possession of an objective, critical intelligence trained on life produced satire, only by obscuring the fact that God is not an ironist but a creator of that life which Sammael, the grandest of all satirists, is dedicated to punishing merely for its being life. With a knowledge of Lewis' literary career, it is hard not to feel that the distance he has come from his early self puts Pullman's journey in eclipse. In *Self Condemned* his glance ranged backwards to *Tarr* and assigned a new and harsher fate to the extraordinary hero whose enemy was life. *The Human Age*, moving on from that pitch of disenchantment with self, can only be more general and thus more hopeful: not only the extraordinary hero, the satirist, but Man himself is on trial.

Lewis' effort to imagine, to invent, to look beyond and make up a story about Man is of more compelling interest than biographical speculations about what the author really believed in his last years. So far as anyone knows, he did not become a Catholic; neither does his hero, James Pullman. For our purposes, what Lewis believed is in the pages of *The Human Age;* and perhaps all they tell us is that the impulse, the gesture, is directed out from the self in an effort at inclusive sympathy and awe—as much as any one might demand of a novelist.

Despite his wishes, it is unlikely that he will be remembered for *The Human Age* more than for his other books; and we may take the Tolstoyan discounting of earlier work not as a final attempt at repentance, but as the inflection of a truly creative artist so engaged in making one more raid on the inarticulate that nothing finished and in the past mattered very much. Lewis died before his most ambitious literary flight—to heaven itself—was completed; yet the book, like his career as a whole, seems anything but unfinished. What more does one ask than to see Pullman carried away by two of God's soldiers? To regret that the outcome is denied us would only be the mark of a reader overzealous to know how Everything turns out. The future was, at the end, as open as it had ever been—the writer, as ready to make his venture.

Notes and References

Chapter One

1. Wyndham Lewis archive, Cornell University.
2. *Ibid.*
3. *English Review* (May 1909).
4. Quoted in Hugh Kenner, *Wyndham Lewis* (New Directions, 1954), p. 15.
5. *The Old Gang and the New Gang* (London, 1933), pp. 16–17.
6. "The Sea Mists of the Winter," *The Listener* (May 10, 1951), p. 765.

Chapter Two

1. Ezra Pound, "Wyndham Lewis," *Little Review*, 1918. Reprinted in *Literary Essays of Ezra Pound*, ed. T. S. Eliot (London, 1954), p. 425.
2. V. S. Pritchett, "The Eye-Man," *Books in General* (New York, 1955), p. 249.
3. T. S. Eliot, "John Dryden," *Selected Essays* (New York, 1949), p. 267.
4. Pritchett, *Books in General*, p. 263.
5. *Egoist*, Sept. 1918. Reprinted in The Wyndham Lewis number of *Shenandoah*, IV, Nos. 2–3, pp. 65–68.

Chapter Three

1. Charles Handley-Read, *The Art of Wyndham Lewis* (London, 1951), p. 40. The whole chronological outline contains much information, though not all of it is accurate.
2. T. S. Eliot, *Selected Essays* (New York, 1932), p. 346, and in *The Use of Poetry and the Use of Criticism* (London, 1933), p. 112.
3. "His pamphleteering volumes are not books; their air of sustained and ordered argument is a kind of bluff . . ." F. R. Leavis, "Mr. Eliot, Wyndham Lewis and Lawrence," *Scrutiny* III, 1934–35 (Cambridge, 1963), 188. "He cannot make words express a precise meaning: he showers the reader with a verbal offensive . . . in the huff-snuff

rhetoric which is a non-occult form of automatic writing:" Northrop Frye, "Neo-Classical Agony," *The Hudson Review* (Winter, 1957–58), 592.

4. Quoted in Walter Allen, "Lonely Old Volcano," *Encounter* XXI, No. 3 (September, 1963), 63.

5. But for Lewis' further responses to Mussolini and Fascism see Geoffrey Wagner, *Wyndham Lewis: A Portrait of the Artist as the Enemy* (New Haven, 1957), pp. 72–74.

6. ". . . *Time and Western Man* still fills my imagination. I have a curiously personal feeling of gratitude. He has found an expression for my hatred—a hatred that being half dumb has half poisoned me. . . . He will have an immense effect—but alas he is so clear the fools will think they understand him and hiss or bray what they have found." *The Letters of W. B. Yeats*, ed. Allan Wade (New York, 1955), p. 734.

7. See R. G. Collingwood, *An Essay on Metaphysics* (Oxford, 1940), Part I.

8. See George Santayana, *Winds of Doctrine* (New York, 1926), pp. 58–109, and Bertrand Russell, *Our Knowledge of the External World* (Chicago, 1929), Chapter 2.

9. Sir Charles Snow mentions *Science and the Modern World* as one of the proofs that "A whole body of literature has been built up over a generation, written, incidentally, in some of the most beautiful prose of our time, to demonstrate the intellectual, aesthetic and moral values inherent in the pursuit of science. . . ." The use of "beautiful" here recalls Lewis' account of Bergson's "saying it with flowers." See *The Two Cultures and a Second Look* (Cambridge, 1964), p. 63.

10. "But 'what we ordinarily call thinking' is just what he is incapable of—consider, for instance, the list of names brought together under the 'Time Philosophy' in *Time and Western Man*." Leavis, *Scrutiny* III, 187.

11. *W. B. Yeats and T. Sturge Moore: Their Correspondence 1901–1937*, ed. Ursula Bridge (New York, 1953), pp. 117–19.

Chapter Four

1. In his essay "The Diabolical Principle" Lewis mocks the protestations of Jolas and Paul, the editors of *Transition*, that they are purely and simply amusing themselves, detached from the world of revolutionary politics.

2. Page references are to be revised (1956) edition of *Childermass*. Actually, with the exception of an added concluding paragraph which leads into *The Human Age*, and a shortening of the title, there are no significant revisions.

3. The tributes from Wells and Yeats are quoted by Mr. Rose in *The Letters of Wyndham Lewis*, ed. W. K. Rose (London, 1963), pp. 180–81. n.

4. Kenner, *Wyndham Lewis*, pp. 97–98.

Chapter Five

1. Lawrence links Lewis with Aldous Huxley in *Phoenix* (London, 1936), p. 271. Lewis couples Lawrence and Sherwood Anderson in *Paleface*.

2. Lewis' sarcastic treatment of D. H. Lawrence in *Paleface* (1929) would not make for much communication between Leavis and Lewis, especially since T. S. Eliot had used Lewis' account by way of criticizing Lawrence. In "Mr. Eliot, Wyndham Lewis and Lawrence," Leavis allows Lewis "undeniable talent" but finds him absolutely unfit to criticize Lawrence. After an intelligent review by Douglas Garman of some minor Lewis books in the early 1930's, Lewis' literary work went unreviewed and unnoticed in *Scrutiny*. Evidently the undeniable talent did not demand much confrontation. In the Richmond lecture, Leavis applies the heroic epithet "brutal and boring" to Lewis; the case seems closed. From material in the Lewis archive at Cornell, it seems that Lewis became angry at Mrs. Leavis for not mentioning him as a useful analyst of contemporary literary culture in *Fiction and the Reading Public* (1932). He spoke of the Leavises either as a late offshoot of the Bloomsbury tree (!) or, in the preface to *Men Without Art* (1934), as an "appendix" of I. A. Richards. After these wild swings, Lewis remained silent.

3. See his retrospectively mellow essay (partly since Pound was in St. Elizabeth's hospital at the time) in *An Examination of Ezra Pound*, ed. Peter Russell (New Directions, 1950), pp. 257–66; and the fascinating account of Eliot in *T. S. Eliot; Symposium* (Chicago, 1949), pp. 24–32. These, plus the accounts of Pound, Eliot, and Joyce in *Blasting and Bombardiering* temper the earlier criticism made of their writings.

4. Leavis "T. S. Eliot's Stature as Critic," *Commentary* (November, 1958) 399–410.

5. Virginia Woolf, *A Writer's Diary* (New York, 1953), pp. 220–224.

6. The story of Frieda and the horse's thighs is told in Dorothy Brett, *Lawrence and Brett* (Philadelphia, 1933), p. 104. In ". . . Love Was Once a Little Boy," Lawrence gives words to a primrose he feels has been anthropomorphized by Wordsworth: "Hey! Bill! get off the barrow!" *The Later D. H. Lawrence*, ed. W. Y. Tindall (New York, 1952), p. 209.

Chapter Six

1. Kenner, *Wyndham Lewis,* pp. 81–85.
2. *Ibid.,* p. 93.
3. *Ibid.,* p. 107.
4. *Ibid.,* pp. 112–13.
5. Writing to Roy Campbell, the original of Rob McPhail in *Snooty Baronet,* Lewis takes pains to dissociate himself from Snooty, calling him an "ill-mannered and lunatic puppet." But, of course, Lewis is apologizing for killing off Rob-Roy while Snooty goes on to success. *Letters,* pp. 205–6.
6. Julian Symons, *The Thirties* (London, 1960), p. 140.
7. George Orwell, "Looking Back on the Spanish War," *Collected Essays* (London, 1961), p. 188.
8. "There's Wyndham Lewis fuming out of sight, / That lonely old volcano of the Right." The phrase occurs in Auden's "Letter to Lord Byron," *Letters from Iceland,* W. H. Auden and Louis MacNeice (London, 1937), p. 233.
9. The matter is taken up in *Rude Assignment,* pp. 216–19, and in a letter to Felix Giovanelli (*Letters,* p. 463) blaming James Burnham for refusing the review.

Chapter Seven

1. John Holloway, "Wyndham Lewis," in *The Charted Mirror* (London, 1960), pp. 128–29.
2. Compare Graham Greene's *The End of the Affair,* which also appeared in 1951. There are even more obvious examples of smooth transitions.
3. "Inside the Whale," in *Collected Essays* (London, 1961), p. 148.
4. Kenner, *Wyndham Lewis,* p. 153.
5. W. K. Rose, *Wyndham Lewis at Cornell* (Ithaca, 1961), p. 16.
6. John Holloway, *The Story of the Night* (London, 1961), p. 146.
7. Accounts of the conversation can be found in "The Devil and Wyndham Lewis," *Gnomon* (New York, 1958), pp. 240–41, and in Kenner's fine eulogy "Stele for Hephaestus," *Poetry* (August, 1957), 306–10.
8. T. S. Eliot, "A Note on *Monstre Gai,*" *Hudson Review* (Winter, 1955), 522–26.
9. Kenner, *Gnomon,* p. 215.
10. See his interesting, if baffling "On Fairy Stories," *Essays Presented to Charles Williams* (Oxford, 1947), particularly pp. 72–75.

Selected Bibliography

PRIMARY SOURCES

The following list of Wyndham Lewis' publications includes the three periodicals he edited and mostly wrote, as well as a few important stories or essays that have not been incorporated into other books. (No attempt has been made to list his graphic productions.) If the work has not been treated in the text, an explanatory note has been added. An asterisk indicates the edition to which page numbers in the text refer. For a much fuller bibliography and check-list, see Geoffrey Wagner's book on Lewis.

American and Cosmic Man. London: Nicholson and Watson, 1948; New York: Doubleday, 1949.

America, I Presume. New York: Howell, Soskin and Co., 1940. Comic fictionalized account of the Englishman's impressions of America.

Anglosaxony: A League That Works. Toronto: Ryerson Press, 1941. Rather dull propaganda for England as sea power and universal democracy, in contrast to Germany.

The Apes of God. London: The Arthur Press, 1930; New York: Robert McBride, 1932.*

The Art of Being Ruled. London: Chatto and Windus, 1926;* New New York: Harpers, 1926.

Blast: Nos. 1 & 2. London: John Lane, the Bodley Head, 1914, 1915. Much of this material is reprinted in *Wyndham Lewis the Artist,* 1939.

Blasting and Bombardiering. London: Eyre and Spottiswoode, 1937.

"Cantleman's Spring-Mate," *Little Review* (October, 1917). Reprinted in *The Little Review Anthology,* ed. Margaret Anderson. New York: Hermitage House, 1953. This short story is an early example of Lewis in full command of a style.

The Childermass: Part I. London: Chatto and Windus, 1928; New York: Covici-Friede, 1928.

Count Your Dead: They Are Alive! or A New War in the Making. London: Lovat Dickson, 1937. A criticism, through dialogue, of England's responses to the Spanish War. An "anti-war" book.

The Demon of Progress in the Arts. London: Methuen, 1954; Chicago: Henry Regnery, 1955. An attack on the contemporary cult of abstract art.

The Diabolical Principle and the Dithyrambic Spectator. London: Chatto and Windus, 1931. Puts together "The Diabolical Principle" from *Enemy* #3, and "The Dithyrambic Spectator" from *The Calendar of Modern Letters*, April, 1925. The former attacks the Joyce-*Transition* cult; the latter discusses the Cambridge anthropological school.

The Doom of Youth. New York: Robert McBride, 1932; London: Chatto and Windus, 1932. In support of its thesis that a "youth-cult" is being created and advertised for political purposes, Lewis makes interesting use of newspaper and magazine stories, headlines, advertisements, etc. The English edition was withdrawn after publication.

"Early London Environment." *T. S. Eliot: Symposium.* Chicago: Henry Regnery, 1949. A portrait of Eliot as Lewis knew him in the second decade of the twentieth century.

"Ezra Pound." *An Examination of Ezra Pound.* Norfolk: New Directions, 1950. Appreciative salute to Pound as man and poet.

The Enemy: A Review of Art and Literature, Nos. 1 & 2. London: The Arthur Press, 1927. No. 3, 1929.

The Enemy of the Stars. London: Desmond Harmsworth, 1932. Lewis' "vorticist" play. An earlier version can be found in *Blast* #1.

Filibusters in Barbary. London: Grayson and Grayson, 1932; New York: Robert McBride, 1932. Record of travels in North Africa in 1931. The English edition was withdrawn after publication.

Hitler. London: Chatto and Windus, 1931.

The Hitler Cult. London: Dent, 1939.

The Human Age. Book I: Childermass. London: Methuen, 1956.
> *Books II and III. Monstre Gai and Malign Fiesta.*
> London: Methuen, 1955.

"Imaginary Letters," *Little Review,* 1917–18. Reprinted in *The Little Review Anthology.* Letters written from "William Bland Burn" to his wife about Russian literature, war, the sexes.

The Jews, Are They Human? London: Allen and Unwin, 1939. The irony of the title is unfortunately missed by readers who don't get behind it to the book.

Left Wings over Europe: or How to Make a War about Nothing. London: Jonathan Cape, 1936. Lewis' political polemic at its most onesided and outrageous: Germany as persecuted and innocent; England as the guilty persecutor.

The Letters of Wyndham Lewis, ed. W. K. Rose. London: Methuen, 1963; New York: New Directions, 1963.

The Lion and the Fox. The Role of the Hero in the Plays of Shake-speare. London: Grant Richards, 1927; New York: Harper, 1927. Reprinted London: Methuen, 1955.*

Men Without Art. London: Cassell, 1934.

The Mysterious Mr. Bull. London: Robert Hale, 1938. Popular exploration of the English character.

The Old Gang and the New Gang. London: Desmond Harmsworth, 1933.

One-Way Song. London: Faber, 1933. Reprinted with an introduction by T. S. Eliot, 1960. Lewis' only volume of poems. Familiar *Enemy* sentiments expressed in rough and ready language.

Paleface: The Philosophy of the "Melting Pot." London: Chatto and Windus, 1929. Most of this material appeared in *Enemy* #3.

"The 'Pole,'" *English Review* (May, 1909). Lewis' first published story.

The Red Priest. London: Methuen, 1956. His last completed novel. Eliot's remark in his eulogy for Lewis that the hero of this novel —an Anglican-Communist Priest—was "preposterous," might be extended to the entire novelistic action.

The Revenge for Love. London: Cassell, 1937. Reprinted, London: Methuen, 1952;* Chicago: Henry Regnery, 1952.

Rotting Hill. London: Methuen, 1951;* Chicago: Henry Regnery, 1952.

Rude Assignment: A Narrative of My Career Up-to-date. London: Hutchinson, 1950.

The Roaring Queen. London: Jonathan Cape, 1936. This novel was withdrawn before publication.

Satire and Fiction, also Have with You to Great Queen Street! The History of a Rejected Review, by Roy Campbell. London: The Arthur Press, 1930. The post-*Apes of God* controversy. "Satire and Fiction" was reprinted as part of *Men Without Art.*

Self Condemned. London: Methuen, 1954; * Chicago: Henry Regnery, 1955.

"Some Innkeepers and Bestre," *English Review* (June, 1909). Another of the earliest stories. Reprinted and altered in *The Wild Body*; the earlier version is even more relaxed and expansive.

"The Sea-Mists of the Winter," *Listener* (May 10, 1951).

Snooty Baronet. London: Cassell, 1932.

Tarr. London: Egoist Press, 1914. New York: Alfred Knopf, 1914.* Revised edition, London: Chatto and Windus, 1928. Reprinted revised edition, London: Methuen, 1951.*

Time and Western Man. London: Chatto and Windus, 1927;* New York, Harcourt, Brace, 1938; Boston: Beacon Paperback Edition,

1957. Incorporates "The Revolutionary Simpleton" from *Enemy* #1.

The Tyro: A Review of the Arts of Painting, Sculpture, and Design, Nos. 1 & 2. London: The Egoist Press, 1921, 1922.

The Vulgar Streak. London: Robert Hale, 1941.

The Wild Body: A Soldier of Humour and Other Stories. London: Chatto and Windus, 1927;* New York: Harcourt, Brace, 1928.

The Writer and the Absolute. London: Methuen, 1952.

Wyndham Lewis the Artist, from "Blast" to Burlington House. London: Laidlaw and Laidlaw, 1939. Reprints *Blast* material and *The Caliph's Design.*

SECONDARY SOURCES

ALLEN, WALTER, "Lonely Old Volcano: The Achievement of Wyndham Lewis," *Encounter,* XXI (September, 1963), 63–70. Review article on the publication of Lewis' letters. Makes out a good case for the high value of his literary career.

CARTER, THOMAS, "Rationalist in Hell," *Kenyon Review,* 18 (Spring, 1956), 326–36. Intelligent review article on *The Human Age.*

ELIOT, T. S., "The Lion and the Fox," *Twentieth Century Verse,* 6–7 (Nov.–Dec., 1937).

———. "A Note on *Monstre Gai,*" *Hudson Review,* 7 (Winter, 1955), 522–26.

———. "Tarr," *The Egoist,* 5 (September, 1918), 105–6. Reprinted in *Shenandoah,* 1953.

———. "Wyndham Lewis," *Hudson Review,* 10 (Summer, 1957), 167–71.

FRYE, NORTHROP, "Neo-Classical Agony," *Hudson Review* (Winter, 1957–58), 592–98. Interesting, mainly adverse criticism of Lewis.

GRIGSON, GEOFFREY, *A Master of our Time: A Study of Wyndham Lewis.* London: Methuen, 1951. Enthusiastic pamphlet on the occasion of Methuen's reprinting of Lewis; written by one of his strongest admirers.

HANDLEY-READ, CHARLES, ed. *The Art of Wyndham Lewis.* London: Faber, 1951. Contains an essay on detail in the artist's style, a chronological outline, and notes on the plates. A critical evaluation by Eric Newton.

HARRISON, JOHN R., *The Reactionaries.* London: Gollancz, 1966. Contains a chapter on Lewis' politics.

HOLLOWAY, JOHN, "Wyndham Lewis: The Massacre and the Innocents." *The Charted Mirror.* London: Routledge & Kegan Paul, 1960. Probably the best single essay on Lewis' work. Praises and describes his "massive or violent insight" into modern reality;

ranks him with the great writers of this century: Yeats, Eliot, Lawrence.

KENNER, HUGH, *Wyndham Lewis*. Norfolk, Conn.: New Directions, 1954. By far the best book on Lewis; puts a high critical estimate on the importance of his writings and shows how they make up a career. In places somewhat overwhelming in manner, it nevertheless repays the closest attention. Lewis himself called it a "splendid study."

————. "The Devil and Wyndham Lewis." *Gnomon*. New York: McDowell-Obolensky, 1958. Excellent discussion of *The Human Age*.

LEAVIS, F. R., "Mr. Eliot, Wyndham Lewis and Lawrence," *Scrutiny*, III (1934–35) Cambridge University Press, 1963, 184–91. Also reprinted in Leavis, *The Common Pursuit*. London: Chatto and Windus, 1952. Hostile criticism of Lewis with almost no particular demonstration. Interesting mainly for the way a strong mind deals with three other strong minds.

PORTEUS, HUGH GORDON. *Wyndham Lewis: A Discursive Exposition*. London: Desmond Harmsworth, 1932. The earliest book on Lewis, now rather outdated.

POUND, EZRA. "*Tarr*, by Wyndham Lewis," *Little Review*, 1918. Reprinted in *Literary Essays of Ezra Pound*, ed. T. S. Eliot. London: Faber, 1954. With Eliot's review, the first important criticism of Lewis.

————. "Augment of the Novel," *New Directions in Prose and Poetry*. Norfolk, Conn.: New Directions, 1941. Unflaubertian character of Lewis performance in *Apes of God*. Treats *Apes* as specimen of the "clodhopping blaring potwolloper." Sloppy but amusing essay.

PRITCHETT, V. S. "The Eye-Man." *Books in General*. New York: Harcourt, Brace and Co., 1955, pp. 248–53. Lewis' novelistic originality held to lie in his use of painterly techniques.

RICKWOOD, EDGELL. "Wyndham Lewis." *Scrutinies* vol. 2. London: Wishart and Co., 1931. Good early assessment of the writer's virtues and limitations.

ROSE, W. H. *Wyndham Lewis at Cornell*. Ithaca, New York: Cornell University Press, 1961. A review of the contents of the Lewis Archive at Cornell.

Shenandoah, 4 (Summer-Autumn, 1953). Wyndham Lewis Number. Reprints Eliot's essays on *Tarr* and the *Lion and the Fox*, also some remarks by Pound. Contains essays by Kenner, Marvin Mudrick, and Marshall McLuhan.

TOMLIN, E. W. F. *Wyndham Lewis*. London: Longmans, Green, 1955. A British Council pamphlet.

Twentieth Century Verse, 6/7 (Nov.–Dec., 1937). Wyndham Lewis Double Number. Lively collection of criticisms, tributes or short statements about Lewis' art and criticism.

WAGNER, GEOFFREY. *Wyndham Lewis: A Portrait of the Artist as the Enemy*. New Haven: Yale University Press, 1957. A mine of information about Lewis with immense bibliography. Often the information swamps the critique, and it is hard to see just what the book's argument looks like. But indispensable for purposes of source or detail.

Index

177